The Journey of Recovery

From Delusion to Truth!

Daily Spiritual Healing Reflections

Pedro Henrique

The Journey of Recovery

Copyright © 2025 Pedro Henrique

All rights reserved.

This book contains original *Daily Reflection* passages for personal meditation, recovery, and well-being. The content is for inspirational purposes only and is not a substitute for professional medical or therapeutic advice.

No part of this book may be copied, reproduced, distributed, or used in any form without prior written permission from the copyright owner, except for brief excerpts used in a book review or educational discussion. For permission requests or inquiries, please contact email: thejourneyofrecovery1999@gmail.com

Thejourneyofrecovery.com

Library of Congress

ISBN: 9798998938504 (Paperback)
ISBN: 9798998938511 (e-book)

Dedication

For the one who stood beside me, steady and silent, as I fought to find my way back to spiritual balance.

Wordlessly—she carried her love, our shared pain, and unwavering support in her gaze and the tenderness of her touch.

Through her quiet strength, she helped me heal and grow—as a man, a father, a son, a friend, and a loving soulmate.

Carla, for your gentle courage and your boundless heart—

I am forever grateful.

The Journey of Recovery

Acknowledgements

To my son, Travis—my pride and my joy. Your very existence *inspires* me to be my best. I love you.

To those who've traveled the path of spiritual recovery before me and left recognizable footprints for me to follow, I bow to you.

To the family members and friends that stood by my side, your unconditional love and validation, are treasures I hold dearly in my heart.

To the Monday night zoom group that originated out of a devastating pandemic and turned into a second family, I thank you.

To my mentor Joe C. and friend Brendan C., who, though thousands of miles away, spent hours on the phone, giving my pain a voice, making space for it, and offering their hearts as refuge. I am blessed to have you in my life.

Thank you to everyone who clicked "like" or left a comment on my posts @myjourneymeditations and on my new page @thejourneyofrecovery1999. Your support and encouragement kept me going.

I would be remiss if I didn't mention Onur B. for the excellent book cover he created, and my dear cousin Valério Ferreira, for the photo on the back cover. I appreciate your professionalism.

Lastly, to Krysta Maravilla, my editor and guide on this project, I am thankful for your patience; it so often calmed my anxieties. Your devotion, talent, and voice as a writer are finding your readers. You are a star in the making. *From Delusion to Truth* may not have come to fruition without your contributions, motivation and belief.

Editor's Note

This is not just a book of daily reflections—it is a living testament to the power of surrender, the grace found in spiritual awakening, and the resilience of the human spirit. Within these pages, you will encounter the raw honesty of a journey from delusion to truth, from despair to healing. Pedro Henrique offers not simply words, but his soul—shared through moments of vulnerability, painful realizations, and spiritual breakthroughs.

These reflections are not bound by calendar dates or linear time. Begin where you are. Return often. Let these words meet you in your moments of struggle, uplift you in times of joy, and remind you—always—that healing is possible, peace is within reach, you are not alone, and love is your truest essence.

This book is a companion for those seeking freedom from the chains of past regrets, the weight of addiction, or the ache of spiritual disconnection. May it serve as a guidepost toward the serenity found in letting go, the courage to embrace your authentic self, and the discovery of the light that resides within you.

With gratitude,

Krysta Maravilla

Stay marvelous.

The Journey of Recovery

Introduction

Writing to the self has been one of the most transformative adventures I've ever embarked on. Each word, a mirror; each sentence, a bridge—not only to who I was, but to who I am becoming.

Shortly after my mother's passing in 2020, I was confronted with unforeseen conflicts that turned my world upside down. I hit a deep emotional bottom.

The gift of desperation visited me for a second time. But, instead of immediately turning to the solution that had once saved me from insanity, I took back my self-will and tried to force an outcome that aligned with my desires. Matters only got worse, and I was brought to my knees.

I began a daily practice of journaling, something I had done in the past, but never with consistency or true intention. This time was different. Each morning, upon awakening, I poured my feelings onto the page. Slowly, I began to sense the words flowing through me were transmissions from a place I didn't fully recognize, yet they brought a deep sense of healing to my hurting heart.

In time, these writings evolved into short reflections I shared with friends. I never intended to accumulate over four hundred of them and certainly had no plan to publish or share them beyond that circle. But as the days passed, I realized that the words flowing onto the page were coming from my inner spiritual guide, a part of me and all of us, where love, peace, and serenity reside.

My connection with this inner wisdom deepened, and I built a relationship with a power that had once been just a concept. Despite being introduced to a spiritual solution for my spiritual malady more than twenty years prior, I only now fully embraced it in daily spiritual practice.

In these 366 reflections, I share intimate glimpses into my journey, introspective memories from childhood, the chaos of active addiction, the vulnerability of early sobriety, and the hard-won resolution that ultimately brought balance and insight to my life as a whole.

Throughout these reflections, I often speak of a Higher Power or Spiritual Guide, because I believe that is where the solution to all my problems lives. I've intentionally used over seventy different synonyms for "God" in the hope that one of them resonates with your own understanding of that which is greater than all of us.

Through this process, I became open to receiving guidance, guidance that led me toward a more principled and purposeful life, one that healed my relationship with myself, with others, and with the universe.

In essence, the reflections I share with you are the story of how I found healing by gradually releasing my self-will, shaped by a delusional mind, and learning to trust the spiritual source within me. It is this inner source that gently guides me to live in Truth.

January 1

A Day For Hope

New Year's Day is filled with hope, a day we mark on our calendar as a time for new beginnings. We set goals and hope that this will be the year we commit to achieving them. Some of us will experience setbacks and put off change for another year.

Each new day is a wonderful gift from our Higher Power. The hope we find on the first day of January is one we can experience every morning upon awakening. The coming year will offer 365 opportunities for new beginnings. On each of them we will want to express our gratitude for this unique human experience.

However, as we begin this New Year, let's allow our minds to plan and dream, with a willingness to accept guidance from our Spiritual Source. In this way, all our resolutions will come to fruition, perhaps not in the way we imagined, but in the way they were meant to be.

January 2

My Journey's Prayer

Oh Great Spirit of the Universe

I am here to be of service, through you, to my fellows

I offer myself as an instrument in your hands

I am open to accepting your creativity in my life

I surrender my old ideas to you

I welcome your divine ideas

I have confidence in you to be my guide

I have confidence that my pursuit of you is safe

I know you created me and my creativity

I ask that my life unfold in accordance with Your Will and not in accordance with my insecurities.

Help me to believe that it is not too late and that I am not too small or too flawed to be healed and made whole by you

Help me to love myself and others

To encourage other's growth as well as my own

And to understand the creative anxieties of others as well as my own

I know I am not alone

I know that I am loved and lovable

Help me to create as an act of worship to you

January 3

Regrets

How challenging it is to wipe away the regrets and guilt of my past.

There are many regrettable choices, but were they "wrong?"

When I take a thorough inventory, I find that my "good" outweighs my "bad". If only my mind would allow me equal time to celebrate all the positive things I've done, instead of focusing so much on the less fortunate moments.

What I call "right and wrong," "good and bad," are merely choices I've made on this human journey. The missed opportunities haunt me. The what-could-have-beens cause me sadness.

The way forward is to accept my past actions, mourn what might have been, and use the grief to fan the flames of a glorious tomorrow.

January 4

Our Great Friend

The first step in connecting with our Great Friend is to accept that there is a power greater than ourselves that guides all organisms. How else would flowers know when to bloom, bears know when to hibernate, or volcanoes know when to erupt? These are events in which man has no part. It follows that there must be a Universal Intelligence orchestrating these phenomena.

We find connection by tuning into the frequency of Spirit. In this way, we become open and attuned to the spiritual messages that are sent to us throughout the day. These have been flowing into our subconscious mind since we were born. The Universal Guidance Survival System connects all that exists in the Universe.

With intentional contemplation, we come into harmony with our Great Friend, and by heeding his spiritual guidance, we overcome life's challenging conflicts.

January 5

Humans Being

"We are not human beings having a spiritual experience; we are spiritual beings having a human experience." - Pierre Teilhard de Chardin

The world has become such that material possessions and human achievements are most revered. We have become Humans Doing rather than Humans Being.

Our lives become more meaningful when we take time to connect with our spiritual inner self, the place where love and understanding reside. This ritual becomes part of our day. A part we don't want to miss.

Worship is as individual as the inner spiritual relationship itself. It can be as simple as taking a moment while in line at the grocery store and giving thanks for everything in our lives. It can be more formal and a deeper experience, setting aside time each day for quiet reflection or meditation.

The idea is to enhance our life experience by increasing our spiritual awareness and connection, resulting in greater love and understanding of ourselves, others, and the world. In this way, our life experience will be less that of a Human Doing and become the richer experience of a Human *Being*.

January 6

This Too Shall Pass

There are moments when the hurt from the weight of the elephant kneeling on my chest is so excruciating that I want to surrender to its dominance. In those moments, I find myself turning to my Higher Power for guidance.

There are moments in life when no human power is able to alleviate the deep sadness and disappointment I experience. It would be easy to blame situations or people for my condition. This is my hurt, and I must accept it as solely mine.

Much love surrounds me as well. Over the years, I have planted seeds of love and peace in the garden of my life. They are in full bloom, showering me with precious positive energy and soothing support that uplifts my spirit, but only when I am open to receive it.

This Too Shall Pass. I have weathered many storms in the past. I will overcome the thunderous noise of my present. I openly share my pain as I share my joy. I know that I am blessed, and as such, I will live my today knowing that I am not alone. I am never alone!

I am loved.

I am love.

I am peace!

January 7

To Be!

The greatest challenge in my life is To Be!

My mind wants to wonder, worry, and screen-write my tomorrow. In its untrained state, the mind cannot accept the concept of being in the now. It bursts with energy at the slightest crisis. Unable to transcend real time, it runs in circles and loops, coming up with different scenarios and endless delusional conclusions for every situation in my life.

To train the mind, we increase our ability to be with the spirit. In Being, the spirit allows life to unfold with little interference. In Being, we are still tasked with resolving each situation as it presents itself in our lives. However, in the state of Being, we allow solutions to come to us. We do not imagine delusional outcomes. We do not waste energy unnecessarily.

After a desert storm, the sand eventually settles in its place without interference. There are storms in our lives that disturb our well-being, and for a time, all our emotions, fears, and regrets temporarily overwhelm us. During these times, we benefit from a state of stillness. Our feelings are not under our control. Like the sands of the desert, they will eventually settle without our intervention.

A great accomplishment is to train the mind To Be!

January 8

The Unknown

The Unknown provides uncertainty, worry, and fear. It interrupts the flow of positive energy to our mental, physical, and spiritual selves.

Being that our life is so filled with unknowns, we must develop a manner of living in which to accommodate the unexpected. One tool is that of living One Day At A Time. This can be difficult for us because we have spent all of our lives in a state of planning. It's beneficial to have an intended direction in life, but we cannot waste precious time in worry or fear that we will not reach our intended objectives. "We make plans and God laughs," is the saying.

Let us not live so rigidly that we miss out on a morning's sunrise or the amazement of a night sky filled with endless bright stars. Let's listen to the singing of the birds or to the burble of a cascading waterfall. Let's be fully engaged and present for each precious life-giving inhale and exhale that we take.

Just for today I will abandon the uncertainty of what's to come and place my energy into this joyous today, all along staying flexible and accommodating the unknowns of tomorrow. I will keep focus on the journey and not on the destination, keeping in mind that happiness and achievement are but the outcome of a life well lived, One Day At A Time.

January 9

Climb Toward Serenity

To be privileged to witness the view, one must first be willing to make the climb. Through deep discomfort, we reach out for help—admitting that, alone, we are not capable of becoming unstuck from old ways of thinking and living that no longer serve us.

We come to encounter a solution. Willingness to embrace a new set of principles sets us on the path—yet our stubborn Will can hold us back. Some remain stuck for a lifetime.

But the fortunate ones—the courageous ones—push through their mental rigidity by accepting guidance. They discover that the only true solution is spiritual inspiration.

To experience serenity of heart and peace of mind, our yin and our yang must move in harmony. To find true calm, we must make the effort to connect with something greater.

For those who accept the challenge and make the climb, a grand view awaits them. They will know light and will experience lasting serenity.

January 10

Sorrow

The sorrow I feel is energy. I can choose to waste it in self-pity, or I channel it into motivation and meaningful action. I cannot change the malice of others, but I have the power to shape my outlook. This can be done with increased faith, courage, and belief that overcoming anything is possible.

Getting out of this dark and gloomy forest is the challenge I face today. Tears flow from my heart, but I know there will be a better tomorrow. There is a Divine Power within that led me out of the depths of darkness of my past. I pray for that Power to lift my soul from the deep pit in which it lies today.

There is no darkness that can eclipse the brightness of the Divine that exists within me.

January 11

Listen for Guidance

There is healthy fear, and there is unhealthy fear. Healthy fear warns me of danger ahead and saves me from disaster in my decision-making. Unhealthy fear cripples my ability to realize my uniquely intended purpose in life.

I lived my life playing it safe. Fear of rejection or failure kept me from pursuing my dreams. I have not taken risks for fear of failure and disappointment. If I continued to live this way, I would remain stuck in doubt.

I can choose to ask for guidance, to believe, and to take action toward realizing my goals. I often do not know what is best, but my Inner Survival Instinct guides me. If I sit ever so quietly, I am provided with purposeful direction. The Universe offers only what is truly meant for me and will not provide what is considered to be selfish, foolish, or harmful.

It takes preparation, belief, and spiritual practice to acquire the simple skill of listening for Divine guidance. Thus far, my dreams have been in black and white, but my spirit holds hope that I do not quit on the bright, colorful dreams that await me in my tomorrow.

Remember we must ask, we must risk without fear, without doubt, and with faith our purpose will be realized.

January 12

Enduring Negativity

After a year of false accusations with no opportunity to defend myself, I went from being respected to being branded dishonest and self-serving by a few malicious family members.

My heart knew differently. My Being knew differently.

Then I remembered feelings are not facts, and the opinions of a few do not make them so. It became a battle against the forces of negativity and evil.

I am grateful that a deep sense of acceptance, forgiveness, and hope fuels my desire to overcome all obstacles. When the temptation arises to act out or to give in to suffering, I am reminded that I don't have to endure alone. I hold fast to the belief that bearing and surviving the never-pleasant difficulties encountered on this journey can bring me closer to my Higher Power—but only if I choose to practice restraint, patience, tolerance, faith, and love.

January 13

Self-Pity

When I take inventory of my life and become open to accepting feedback from my Inner Spiritual Guide, I become aware of character flaws that persist in their commitment to protect my ego. In my morning reflection, I became aware of self-pity. I had gone too far in sharing my thoughts and feelings, and had crossed the line in trying to get others to help me carry my pain. This was burdensome and selfish.

Sharing with others *is* a positive action. Yet, demanding their attention or burdening them with my negativity, pushes them away. They begin to feel a sense of helplessness in their inability to take away my suffering.

This is an ineffective and even destructive tool that my inner child uses to feel loved. Rather than feeding the monster by constantly talking about and reliving a negative experience, at times, it would be best to work on releasing it.

Others cannot take away our pain, nor should they feel burdened to help carry our cross. Living a solution-based life and taking action to overcome unpleasant situations is the only way to mitigate our hurt.

Living in a state of gratitude lifts the shadow that self-pity casts over our lives.

January 14

The Power Of Possibility

Each day offers a new start, a new beginning, a new opportunity to transcend the past and awaken to new visions. Only fear can hold me back from connecting to the flow of the Power of Possibility.

My burdened mind, heavy and filled with a lifetime of society's constructed thinking, struggles against change. The Eternal Heart cries out for risks to be taken. There are dreams to live and challenges to overcome.

The Power of Faith is the only adversary powerful enough to stand in the way of fear. I have awakened to my purpose. I often forget that I am the son of the Supreme Divine Master of the Universe; as such, I have within me enough faith to climb the highest mountain and reach my intended destination.

This day offers me yet another opportunity to lace up my boots, to step over fear, and resume my spiritual trek to the summit.

Change is all there is. Nothing is permanent. With faith, anything is possible.

January 15

The Conditioned Mind

My ego-driven mind tries to protect me from life's responsibilities or unpleasant situations. It offers me the choice of being manipulative, dishonest, or evasive to avoid negative consequences. This option may work for a while, but avoiding the inevitable only gives it more power, and eventually, what was a molehill becomes a mountain.

When I began to live a principled life, these same situations were easily overcome by honestly showing up for life. What I called a choice was not a conscious choice at all, but the result of conditioning of the mind during my dysfunctional years.

Spiritual practice awakens consciousness so that those of us who previously lived unprincipled lives emerge to live in Truth, sincerity, and honesty.

January 16

Cherishing Our Inner Being

We tend to take care of our outward appearance, but we don't spend enough time, or in most cases, any time, nurturing our inner being. By not doing so, we spend a lifetime ignoring what is the nature of our joy and peace.

If we made a conscious effort to connect with our Higher Self, we would come to experience the Light that is our essence. We can do this by practicing meditation. It is in the quiet moments that we can detach from mental delusion, judgment, resentment, envy, and worry.

I would like to challenge you to take five minutes for yourself today. Find a quiet place where you will not be disturbed. Sit comfortably with your feet grounding you to the earth. Take deep, gentle inhales that reach the bottom of your lungs. Be present, still, and aware with each exhalation. Eventually, you will begin to experience relaxation of your entire body and mind.

With continued practice, you will begin to experience moments of separation from thought and a sense of calm and peace will wash over you. Dismiss all excuses and rationalizations and commit to these five minutes, even if it is just for today.

The Buddha once said, *"He who is mentally concentrated sees things according to reality." (SN XXII. 5.*

January 17

Accept and Forgive

Divine Master, I'm afraid of the consequences I'll have to bear for actions I have taken. You alone know my heart and know that there was no malice in the choices I made. I own these wrongs regardless of their intent and mourn their undesirable outcome. I ask for your guidance.

My son, I am by your side. This will be an opportunity for you to face and overcome your past. The punitive judgment of others and the consequences that may not fit the wrong, must be both accepted and forgiven. Hold your head high, look adversity in the eye and speak your Truth. I assure you there will be light on the other side of darkness.

And so, it came to be!

January 18

The Natural Flow Of The Spirit

On this day, I will consciously step out of the Ego and tune into The Natural Flow of Spirit. This is found in the now, in mindfulness. The flow cannot be seen, touched, smelled, tasted, or heard. It is spiritual energy, an experience beyond consciousness.

It is often called instinct by some and divine inspiration by others. Both offer guidance. The difference between the two is that instinct is a mental impulse; divine inspiration is a whisper from the Eternal Heart.

To let go of fear or resentment brought about by my ego, I tune my inner dial to the frequency of The Natural Flow of Spirit. The Eternal Heart will guide me to the peace and serenity I seek and humbly carry me through another day.

January 19

Self-Confidence

When I run a marathon, I awaken my survival instinct to fight the forces of doubt and negativity that arise in my mind. I silence doubt and negativity and gain mastery over them by committing to taking one more step. This signals to them that my self-confidence and determination will carry me to my intended goal. I do not surrender to unwelcome chatter.

There are times in life when I find myself on a difficult path. I feel doubt, and although I push on, I experience increased and persistent inner turmoil. This is a time to pause, become aware of what is happening within me, and listen for direction from my Inner Spiritual Guide.

When I feel joyful, calm, realized, useful, or hopeful, it signals that I am on the intended path. When I feel melancholy, anxiety, disappointment, or fear, it signals that I am on a perilous path and need to change course.

Self-confidence is created by constant commitment to spiritual guidance and can be found when I unite my will with that of the Unseen Spiritual Source of the Universe.

Self-confidence and determination dispels doubt from my life.

Removing the Mask

When I am spiritually wounded, I am more likely to compare myself to others. I vacillate between not measuring up (low self-esteem) or having an inflated sense of self (ego-centeredness). Neither serves me well.

Both low self-esteem and ego-centeredness have the ability to hijack my uniqueness, my Truth, my individuality. I become an actor on the grand stage of life, switching between being a people pleaser or an insufferable egomaniac. I hide behind a mask that, if removed, would expose my vulnerability and shatter my false pride.

When I am spiritually whole, I renounce the mask and find the freedom to live outside the delusional notion that the world is judging or evaluating my worth.

Spiritual healing is found in the humility to accept that my humanity is completely imperfect, only then can I take off the mask and allow myself to be what the universe Truly intended me to be.

January 21

Outward Search For Connection

"When you look to God for strength to face responsibility and are quiet before Him, His healing touch causes the Divine Quiet to flow into your very being." Author unknown

From the start, mankind's desire for security, courage and well-being has led him to an outward search for a Supreme Being that possessed perfect power, wisdom and goodness.

Man did not encounter the outcome he desired, and so he distanced himself from spiritual endeavors and began to rely on his deceptive mind to solve the unyielding riddles of life.

We do not need to look outward to find Divine Power. Its infinite wisdom lies within us. The first steps in experiencing spiritual connection involve quieting our mind. This can be achieved by practicing deep-breathing meditation with the faithful intention of engaging our inner spirit. Through repetition, intention and wishful belief, we will begin to experience a healing sensation.

The power of meditation is a unique experience available to all of us. Although the methods of finding stillness may vary, the end result will be a healing connection with our Guiding Spirit.

January 22

Stillness of Mind

The Master whispers that I reflect on my inner spiritual condition and detach from the material external condition. External Conditions are impermanent and ever changing. The inner spirit will remain present to love me and pick up the pieces of hurt that fall to the cold hard ground.

Serenity can be found in those all-too-rare moments when external and inner conditions align. In these moments, the turbulent waters of emotion become calm and the howling wind of fear becomes still.

It is in moments of despair that most individuals seek contact with the Unseen Power. It is when we experience deep suffering that we consider opening the gates of our heart and allowing for spiritual guidance. In the Stillness of Mind, we will hear His soothing message. It will bring comfort to the painful situations we alone create.

January 23

The Guardrails

I wonder what it would be like to cross a bridge without guardrails. I imagine it would be similar to living a life devoid of spiritual guidance.

When I cross a bridge, I hardly pay attention to the railings, but they are there to keep me from going over the edge. Without the rails, the experience would be very different. I wouldn't feel safe, and the crossing would be filled with debilitating dread.

Get across it we must, if we're to get to the other side.

The bridge is the dash between the beginning and the end of our human experience. The guardrails are the Divine Guide that provides the security we need to navigate all the obstacles we face on our human journey. Without spiritual guidance, I would feel unsafe and live in fear. Fear manifests itself as anger, resentment, envy, greed, self-pity, and many other character defects.

As I develop, understand, and expand my spiritual relationship with the Great Reality, I become aware of the guardrails along my journey.

I begin to feel safe and free from fear.

I feel protected from going over the edge.

I become confident that I will survive the crossing and arrive safely at the intended destination, the place of Eternal Peace.

January 24

The Alternate Route

On the journey of life, the intended destination is to the land of happiness and peace. The process should be filled with calm and joy, like a slow drive on a scenic, winding country road.

We have built highways and byways, bridges and tunnels to accommodate our fast-paced lives. We've become reckless, and inevitably, there's a crash that sends drivers on a detour through unfamiliar rural roads.

For most, this will be their first ride through the tranquil countryside. Were it not for the crashes, most would never experience The Alternate Route.

Eventually, the opportunity to jump back on the highway presents itself, and most are eager to pick up where they left off. Some, however, are tempted by the new experience of The Alternate Route. They welcome the peaceful calm and choose a new way of life. Their lives are forever changed.

I no longer feel safe at high speeds, and I've chosen not to tempt the dangers of reckless roadways. It's on a quiet country road, in my humble clunker, that I feel most at peace. Today, I choose to live at a slower pace—on the Alternative Route.

January 25

Spiritually Fit

A Spiritual Fit Person is one who accepts their imperfect self, all other beings, and the universe exactly as they are. They understand that everything is interconnected—that we are all part of one shared experience. We are part of each other, and the universe is part of us all.

Being Spiritually Fit does not mean that we are members of a religious order, nor does it mean that we must meditate, pray, or howl at the moon. These may be part of our daily practice, but they don't necessarily mean that we are Spiritually Fit. One can participate in none of the above and be a Spiritually Fit individual.

Being Spiritually Fit does mean that our thoughts and actions toward ourselves, others, and the universe are free of malice. It means that we practice patience, tolerance, and acceptance in all our affairs. It also means that when our imperfections prevail on any given day, we acknowledge our wrongdoing, immediately apologize for our action, and repent.

When we are Spiritually Fit, we lack resentment or jealousy because our love, joy, and gratitude overflow. We are free of regret because we are honest and respectful of our family, friends, neighbors, co-workers, and all others with whom we interact.

Living by these humble principles does not eliminate our imperfect humanity. But it does bring us infinite peace and renders us Spiritually Fit.

January 26

Give What You Have

Early in life, I sought center stage, the leading role. It was an effort to get his attention. I craved his guidance, his love, and his approval. I was dependent on external conditions and blind to the existence of an inner spirit that resides within. The person from whom I craved this love could not give that which they did not have.

I settled for the affection of those who benefited from my self-serving altruism. This filled the void, but only for a moment, for soon, the hunger demanded more.

There were also people who genuinely loved me, but because my own cupboards were bare, I was unable to return their love in kind. I could not give that which I did not have.

It was only after I awakened to the Infinite Divine Source of Love within me that I began to love others sincerely, without expectation or demand.

People will fail us, but the Master's love is pure and always present.

January 27

Divine Consciousness

We are heading toward self-destruction. The only way to slow our momentum is to awaken to a shared Divine Consciousness—an awareness that we are all spiritually connected. We must come to the Divine Truth that we share the same Parent and live beneath the same roof.

The world must be awakened from the trance it is in. The light of love must shine.

As individuals walking a spiritual path, we carry a sacred obligation—to spread the message of peace. One soul, one voice, whether yours or mine, can begin the ripple that carries this message across the globe.

It can all start with us.

Let us then begin by sharing peace with those around us through selfless love. For true love is only found in a way of life that, above all else, cherishes peace—for all our brothers, all our sisters, all beings.

January 28

Higher Thought

We had no choice, for we were ignorant of the existence of Higher Thought. Higher Thought is God's Will for us.

We welcome the Great Spirit into our lives and connect with Him in moments of quiet communion. In this way, we are guided toward principled living. Our gifts grow in importance while our challenges decrease in significance.

The struggles of life do not disappear. Yet, our conflicts diminish. We'll stop asking, "Why did this happen to me?" and ask, "What can I learn from this lesson, Father? "

We cease to bow to the self-centeredness of our ego and become more patient, accepting, and forgiving. These qualities enrich our character. We seek only that our will and the Will of God, as we understand Him, coexist in harmonious union.

Ego-based living breeds restlessness. By living by the Will of the Divine Power for Good in the World, we come to know peace.

Thy Will not mine be done.

January 29

The Good Guy

Years ago, when I entered recovery battered and bruised, clueless, and alone, I met a gentle man who spoke softly and had a remarkable ability to listen. The feelings I was experiencing and sharing with him were reflected back to me in his tender eyes. I felt his presence in every word I spoke. When I finished, he paused and responded: "Pedro, you're a good guy."

On several occasions, he took me to Rikers Island Correctional Facility to share my story of recovery with inmates incarcerated for crimes related to their addictions. He was a humble servant. At the end of each of our visits, he would gently hug each of the young inmates and say to each of them, softly, almost in a whisper, "Remember, you're a good guy." They would smile, not knowing how to respond. I knew how they felt; his words affected me the same way every time he said them to me.

I wanted to have what he had; his calm, his kindness, and his kind words. He was instrumental in the career path I chose for my journey. His spirit now resides on a higher plane, no doubt close to his Higher Power, which he chose to call God. On this day, he will celebrate another sober anniversary.

Happy Anniversary my friend, and thank you for being The Good Guy.

January 30

Sincerity Through Vulnerability

Vulnerability is not a sign of weakness; it is the ability to bare our Truth. The other option is to live with a veil of insincerity.

Often, it is easiest to pretend, to play a role, so that others will not judge us as weak. Eventually, we get lost in the dramas of our lives and lose track of who we really are. Sadly, some live their entire lives in character, hidden behind the veil, never knowing who they were meant to be.

It takes courage to become vulnerable. We risk the judgment of others. We may feel rejected because people are threatened by our honesty. Reality has a hard time fitting into a world where delusion is rampant.

By becoming vulnerable, we become honest with ourselves, honest with others, honest with the world. We share our thoughts without fear of retribution. We say what we mean and mean what we say.

We don't seek popularity, we favor sincerity!

January 31

Distract the Past

To live in the now, to be present in this moment, is to live in reality. Unfortunately, the pleasant memories of our past are often distracted by the negative experiences whose hurt cannot be undone. The best we can do is find acceptance for what has passed. Sometimes, it feels like it was all a dysfunctional dream. It is not so!

Every new relationship and situation should be approached as a blank slate, unbiased and pure. We must not allow past negative memories or future projections to pull us away from reality and into delusion. Doing so impedes the natural flow of present or future results.

We can turn to our Higher Self, the non-judgmental part of our humanity, for guidance each time we are about to enter what we anticipate will be a challenging situation. In this way, we will distract the past, if only for a moment, and allow for present reality to take center stage.

Living today's reality Distracts us from the Past!

The Journey of Recovery

February 1

Being Purposeful

Being valued is necessary for our spiritual survival, without it, we may not perish, but we will live purposeless lives. Most important is that we value ourselves. That we accept our imperfection and strive daily to correct our mistakes. All feelings, emotions, victories, and losses are an inside job; we have the ability to interpret our shortcomings and successes.

Once we've taken an honest inventory of our lives, we'll be able to assess what we have and what we need to feel fulfilled. Our primary purpose is to be productive members of society.

Being Purposeful requires action, effort, desire, and work. When we lack direction, we reach out for guidance. When we lack inspiration, we connect with our Divine Consciousness and seek insight from the Unseen Spirit.

When we value and contribute to the tribe, the tribe, in turn, values and contributes to us. Being Purposeful renders us spiritually whole.

February 2

Dancing With Emotion

We all experience emotional threats to our well-being. Whether they are financial, familial, social, or physical, they deserve our full attention. Although we reach into our spiritual toolbox and apply every resource available, sometimes the threat does not go away. For that moment, a tidal wave of confusion thunders over our otherwise peaceful state of mind. These moments are rare, but very real and very frightening.

In these times, it is useless to ignore such a persistent emotion, instead of confronting it, we should welcome it. No arguments or debates. Even though the message of our emotion is hurtful, we listen to it. After hearing its message, we put on some soft music and dance with it, we make peace, we come to terms. When the ritual is complete, we escort it to the door and say a peaceful goodbye.

We then thank the Almighty for the experience, for it has given us the awareness that we possess the resilience to once again overcome the seemingly overwhelming threat of our most complex emotions.

February 3

Control

There are situations that create feelings of helplessness. Some time passes, the unwanted feelings move on, and we take time to reflect. It becomes clear that they were related to our lack of control because when we are in a similar situation and in charge, we do not feel such powerlessness.

When we are in control, we command our feelings, emotions, and actions. The problem is that control is a fickle friend. These are matters of the material world. The world of the Spirit does not depend on control as a means of emotional survival; our challenging moments are embraced as opportunities for growth.

When we allow ourselves to be guided by the Spirit of the Universe, we give up our dependence on control. We go with the flow of life, offering little resistance or meaning to the natural challenges we face. We come to believe that everything happens for a reason. There is a lesson to be learned from all our experiences. The pleasant and the unpleasant are both wise professors.

Our complicated emotional states become less frequent as we surrender to the fact that life follows an intuitive course. It refuses to bend to our will. We have a choice: either we let go of our control or we are dragged by it.

February 4

Gifting Compassion

Our ego can become possessive of our compassion, clinging to it as if it were something to be owned. But this attachment only leads to spiritual restlessness—for it is in the act of giving, freely and without condition, that we find our greatest joy.

Sometimes, all we have to offer is compassion. And that alone is enough. But when we lock compassion away in our hearts, we deprive others of a gift more precious than gold. To possess our compassion—to withhold it—is to place an obstacle in our path toward oneness with the Divine and with each other. The gift of ourselves—our presence, our love, our understanding—will always matter more than any material offering.

Giving compassion is being fully present for someone. Allowing their thoughts or feelings a voice when they would otherwise be silenced. This could be our homebound grandmother who lives alone, our partner whom we often take for granted, or our child who sometimes goes unrecognized. We experience increased value when we offer such consideration.

By offering our Compassion, we repay the blessings humbly bestowed upon us by our Higher Power.

February 5

Today's Peace

If I allow it, the selfish choices of the past will rob me of today's peace. Today offers the opportunity to make choices that will gift serenity to the future. All that has meaning happens in the now. If I allow myself to drift into my long-ago yesterdays or distant tomorrows, I willfully ignore the blessings of today.

At this moment, I have everything I need: enough health, enough shelter, enough love, enough food, enough worry, and enough faith. My reality is not in yesterday or tomorrow.

In prayer and meditation, I bring awareness to the present moment and offer gratitude to the All-Powerful for the blessings that have been bestowed upon me.

It is only in this way that I can again claim Today's Peace.

February 6

The Usual Suspects

Control is Ego-based. It is introduced into conscious thought by its partner in crime, the Mind. They are the usual suspects involved in robberies of peace and serenity.

These conniving, stealing thieves are dedicated to their destructive mission. They come disguised as wise men, bearing gifts of prestige and prosperity. Their plans lack consideration. Their vice is power and control. Unsuspecting of their dastardly plan, we become hypnotized by their deception.

To avoid an attack on our spiritual vault, we need to install a round-the-clock security system. Vigilantly taking inventory of our spiritual condition keeps us modest. When we identify resentment, fear, self-pity, judgment, intolerance or greed, we quickly sound the alarm and call upon humility to the rescue.

For the best protection, we put the Great Unseen Power in charge of our will. In this way, we have an impenetrable protector of our humility from the forces of The Usual Suspects.

February 7

The Hurdle of Faith

To connect with a Power Greater Than Ourselves, we must first cultivate a sincere desire for spiritual knowledge. Once we've awakened to this longing, we've cleared the high hurdle of faith, a leap few dare attempt, for most are afraid to embark on a path of pure Truth, fearing the unraveling of familiar comforts.

This spiritual journey often begins with doubt, evolves into uncertainty, gradually blossoms into curiosity and leads to the manifestation of a relationship with our Unknown Friend.

Some of us had to suffer excruciating mental and emotional pain before reluctantly reaching out to the Spiritual Source. We crawled to the door of desire, arriving with bloodied knees.

We do not need to experience suffering before reaching out to the Eternal Heart. We only need surrender to overcome the Hurdle of Faith.

February 8

Resolving Inner Turmoil

I spent a lot of time contemplating a situation that caused me great emotional conflict. I felt that my rights, my reputation, and my safety had been violated. It consumed me to the point of dark emotional despair. Sleepless nights and days filled with doubt and fear lasted for months.

I placed the individuals involved on trial and found them guilty. The trial took place in my disturbed mind. They were found guilty before a thorough moral investigation. I looked at every angle, trying to gain an advantage and desperately trying to gain control of the situation. It almost drove me mad.

I failed to use the tools available for resolving inner turmoil; I refused to accept the advice of others, and my prayers were not of pure intention. I expected my Higher Power to dispense justice and right this wrong. My Higher Power is not a judge, jury, or restorer of life situations.

I redirected my prayers and found the spiritual solution in the St. Francis prayer, specifically in the phrase: *"It is in forgiving that one is forgiven."* I began to pray for forgiveness for the wrongs of those who had hurt me and for any part I had contributed to the situation. After continued use of the prayer, I became willing to forgive them and myself. Through forgiveness, I resolved this emotional conflict and regained my peace.

February 9

Selfless Understanding

The solution to resolving conflict with another is rooted in humility. It is in the willingness to communicate my feelings openly, rather than engage in a senseless, hurtful tug-of-war, that true resolution can be found.

I choose to avoid picking an unwinnable quarrel, even when I feel I am in the right. There are few absolute rights or wrongs in life, and no true winners or losers. To cling to rigid ways of thinking is to inevitably cause harm both to myself, and to others. The answer to life's relational challenges lies in Selfless Understanding and honest communication.

By forgiving another, I also forgive myself. In this act, I bring peace to us both. Though the damage caused by conflict cannot be fully undone, I can choose to unite with the individual in love and work through the emotional wreckage.

February 10

The Path of Least Resistance

I freely gave up my power and chose the path of service. I chose to be submissive rather than offensive, to remain silent rather than give voice to my pain.

Being of service is not always about action—it can also mean refraining from doing something that would cause harm to another. Sometimes, the most loving service is restraint, even when our hearts are aching to speak.

I remained passive as my character came under attack, but inside me, anger and resentment began to grow. In silence, they festered—until the weight of these feelings became unbearable and unacceptable. From the depths of my pain, delusional thoughts of vengeance began to rise, whispering in the places where peace had once lived.

Revenge would have been a dark, cowardly choice whose only result would have been to feed a lasting resentment.

The many miles traveled on the spiritual path prepared me to overcome the inner torment by drawing closer to the Divine Master and allow Him to guide my actions. Slowly my mind began to calm. Choosing the Path of Least Resistance does not eliminate the pain, but it does increase tolerance.

Though I can still feel the embers of injustice burning deep within me, for one more day I choose service and remain on the path the Master has laid out for my journey.

There are many lessons to be learned and many seasons to be endured on the Path of Least Resistance.

February 11

The Wiser Self

As I grow older, my perspective on life continues to shift. I carry regret for the choices I've made, yet I also hold deep gratitude for the successes and lessons along the way. There are moments when I long for the mistakes of the past to be wiped clean, but I'm learning to accept that even those missteps are part of the story that shaped me.

What is done cannot be undone and what is said cannot be unsaid. If I had not known pain, how could I have come to know joy? The sourness of failure makes success a welcome sweetener.

When I am willing to forgive my younger self for the misfortunes, the missteps, and the bold, naïve bravado of years gone by, I find gratitude. Gratitude for the lessons learned, the strength gained, and the journey that shaped who I am today.

I thank you, Master, for all you have shown me.

My past led me to this older, Wiser Self.

February 12

The Light of the Spirit

A pure heart alone does not shield the mind from selfish or unwelcome thoughts.

The conflicts between good and evil, the pull between the material and the spiritual, often unsettles our peace. Yet I pray that our intention, rooted in unconditional love, may rise above the malice that seeks to invade our minds.

As our connection to the goodness of the Spirit deepens, we become less tolerant of exterior intrusions. Serenity is in the heart, but society's unpredictability and accumulation of ill intentions drain energy from our soul.

It will not always be like this. I believe the season will change. I sense that the Master still has lessons to teach us. Perhaps increasing darkness and pain will motivate humility and purify our world. Perhaps we are doomed to a fiery end.

We will find hope in detachment from earthly thinking. The practice of unconditional love toward one another will promote peace. We lift our hearts to the will of The Divine Force For Good in the world, who has all power. Through his guidance, we will keep our hearts pure and pray to be illuminated by the Light of the Spirit.

February 13

Avoid the Unforgivable

It is harmful to any relationship when we hide our feelings out of fear of hurting our partner. By avoiding honest communication, we create distance and misunderstanding.

To avoid the hurtful words that can erupt from buried resentment, we must take the courageous step of expressing our feelings as they arise, once they've been gently filtered for malice or blame. When we suppress emotions, even the smallest grievances can quietly accumulate. And all too often, they surface in moments of tension, misdirected and magnified, harming those we care about most.

When we open ourselves to communicate the entirety of our feelings—free from doubt or hesitation, we set a powerful intention. We begin to live from a place of purity of heart, where Truth and love guide our words. In doing so, we cultivate serenity and protect ourselves from the deep wounds that come from silence, bitterness, or betrayal. We live in a way that helps us Avoid the Unforgivable.

February 14

God is Love

If the word God causes you confusion or discomfort, replacing it with the word Love will make it easier to understand God.

Love is in everything. Everything created by Love is of absolute perfection. We see Love and goodness in all of nature because it remains pure.

Through our insecurities, we develop envy, anger or greed and introduce evil into the world. If we could see Love in one another, our prejudices would melt, and our compassion would grow. If we knew the Love within us, we would be free from all our fears.

Only when we accept the guidance of Love will we experience inner peace and ultimately be at peace with the world.

February 15

Letting Go

Letting go removes the barrier that prevents me from experiencing the serenity I seek. I recognize the need to release the importance I give to my yesterdays and unpredictable tomorrows.

As I embrace the gifts of the present and give thanks that all my needs are met, if only for this day, the bright star of gratitude shines through the haze of mental deception.

When I am fully present in the now, I flow effortlessly through life like a leaf blowing in the wind on a gentle fall day.

February 16

Contradict the Mind

To contradict the mind is our greatest challenge because the mind has the power to override its own logical solutions. But unless we contradict the mind, we cannot engage the spirit. Without engaging the spirit, healing cannot begin and our condition worsens.

In moments of despair, we reach out for help. We may come to accept our spiritual malady as the source of suffering that has plagued us for so long. We learn about a solution and want it for ourselves.

For our healing we are presented with a simple plan of action. Yet, some remain unable to contradict a mind that refutes a spiritual solution and again chooses to embrace the status quo with suffocating force.

Doing the same thing over and over with the expectation of a different result is often referred to as the definition of insanity.

Recovery requires logic, yet logic knows little of recovery.

February 17

Spiritual Blindness

My illusory search for happiness through material means led to my acting out and eventually to inevitable inner turmoil. I lived and loved recklessly. The whirlwind continued into adulthood, causing irreparable damage to myself and all that stood in my way.

The clock does not go back in time.

What has been done cannot be undone.

It is all in the past.

Amen!

I did not know what I did not know, and I have slowly come to let go of guilt and remorse. I came to willingly accept the consequences of my Spiritual Blindness. Today, I am filled with gratitude for the wisdom that accompanied this human experience and for the resilience of my spirit.

I believe the best is yet to come. For, as I come closer to living His Will for me, I also come closer to understanding that *"it is in giving that I receive, and it is only by forgiving that I will be forgiven."* St. Francis

Every chapter of life offers a lesson, and there are many chapters yet to come.

February 18

Be the Change

Man is out of tune with his spiritual reality, does not trust what he cannot see, and can only appreciate material objects. His happiness comes from accumulation, which gives him a very real sense of dominance. His strength and his solution are to exert his power.

The number of people without safety and security is growing every day. They're being left with the crumbs of society. Their human rights and basic needs are slowly being taken away. As material wealth increases, spiritual wealth decreases. Humanity is experiencing a division.

There are few who live by or honor Spiritual Intelligence. For the most part, it is those who have experienced enduring tragedy. With nowhere else to turn, we were forced to get down on our knees and seek guidance to overcome our pain.

Perhaps in the not-too-distant future, our world will be brought to its knees. As our social classes divide us, as we slowly destroy each other and our planet, we will ultimately have to atone for our sins. On that day, after terrible human loss, we will all pray as one.

On this day, let us Be the Change and do our part by sharing our peace. Our impact may not be immediately apparent, but we will not be discouraged. For our efforts, we will receive the Master's blessing.

.

February 19

Guidance and Protection

Although I have an open channel to my Spiritual Guide, I am most sincere in prayer during times of emotional upheaval. During these times, my devotion is deeper. Times of prayer interrupt the negative, delusional thinking that accompanies unfortunate circumstances. In my prayers, I ask the Boundless Divine Power, "What is it that you would have me learn from this hardship?"

Subsequent to prayer, patience is necessary to allow the mysteries of life to unfold. Looking back on my life, all my unpleasant times have borne fruit. That is, I've learned from each suffering. Sometimes, the disturbance lasts longer. Sometimes, the pain is worse. Sometimes, I just want to give up. So far, I have overcome all difficulties, and with each one, my faith and understanding have grown stronger.

We need not wait for adversity to enter into communion with our Spiritual Guide. We must take advantage of his total availability to us and allow his light to show us the way. I will hold his hand and try not to let go, not even for a moment, because my inner child needs constant Spiritual Guidance and Protection on this human journey.

February 20

My Faith

The experiences of our early years shape our belief system. We mirror what we observed in our families, our culture, and society. These impact every next decision we make.

It is unfortunate that few are offered Spiritual Knowledge. I am not referring to religion. There has been and still is much tragedy being caused in the name of "God." Spirituality is without doctrine; it is pure intention, pure love, not influenced by egocentric states of mind.

Only after much emotional pain was I brought to my knees. In recovery, I came to understand and began to practice spiritual principles. In the days in which I did not want to flip to the next page, fearing what was to come, I hung on to a firm belief that what was unbearable today would be used for a better outcome tomorrow.

When my mind becomes dark and confused, my spirit guides me to the light.

We are meant to live safe, peaceful, loving lives.

This is My Faith!!

February 21

The Divine Third

Our ability to feel mixed emotions is part of our humanity. Positive emotions come from love, negative emotions come from ego. Love arises from Pure Spirit, while resentment is caused by dis-ease of the mind.

Pure Spirit arises from our connection with the Divine, for there can be no hate here. The ego serves little purpose in the process of love. It is primarily concerned with measuring up to, or surpassing delusional societal ideals. The insecurities we feel, caused by comparing ourselves to others, have their origin in the ego.

It is understood that we all have basic material needs such as food, water, and shelter. We all share the same desire for material comfort, and hard work should be rewarded. Achievements should be recognized. The ego, when kept in check, can be useful in motivating us to great accomplishments that benefit the entire human race.

The Divine Third provides equilibrium between Pure Spirit and Ego. In this way, the Divine and the material coexist without jealousy or greed.

February 22

Acceptance and Action

Where I am in my life is not where I want to be!

I have two choices when faced with this dilemma. Sink into self-pity or find acceptance of my current situation while developing faith that by taking action, I will create change.

Action can mean changing the external; moving to a new place, ending or beginning a relationship, starting a different career. While these physical changes can offer temporary relief or new perspective, they rarely bring lasting peace on their own. Because no matter where I go, or what I do, I always bring myself along.

Action may involve changing my Spiritual Condition. This can take the form of engaging in prayer, meditation, or positive affirmations. I reframe my perspective by developing a lasting relationship with a Higher Power. My focus shifts from the "inherent I" to the "spiritual inner self."

The process of change begins with an inner spiritual solution. Allowing for spiritual guidance may not bring me to where I want to be, but it will bring me closer to where I ought to be.

February 23

The Real Self

We are in a constant search for our Real Self. This implies that there is a present self that masks our original being. We all wear masks that hide who we really are. Others only see what we allow them to see.

Somewhere along the line, our human experience took precedence over our spiritual journey. We blindly followed a script written for us by society's expectations, or perhaps we were tricked into living someone else's dream.

Some subconsciously come to the realization that they cannot live up to expectations and find refuge in addiction or another maladaptive behavior. Some sleepwalk through their entire life living another's dream. Others simply go mad.

Then there are those who begin a process of spiritual recovery and set out in search of their Truth. Along the way, they continually shed the masks of the many scenes and roles they have played on the stage of life.

The spiritual journey involves attempting to reconcile our past with our present, shredding all scripts in favor of a spiritually guided Real Self.

February 24

The Gift of Sobriety

In the midst of a peaceful day, my mood can quickly be soured by someone else's meaningless comment or action. This creates inner turmoil, exaggerates the situation, and disrupts my precious peace.

These moments remind me that the voice of the ego and its insatiable self-centered appetite are still renting space within the confines of my mind.

To interrupt disturbing thoughts, I turn to my Higher Power and, in a moment of prayer, give thanks for His Gift of Sobriety. Without it, the ego leads my mistrust to misguided impulsive reactions with unfortunate consequences.

Gratitude disarms the ego and restores spiritual balance to its rightful throne.

February 25

Trusting the Inexplicable

The universe is full of unexplainable mysteries. We all share a life force, an energy that ensures the survival of all living organisms. This spiritual energy guides me. It guides us all. It exists on a level higher than mind or thought.

When overwhelmed, I find refuge in the idea that this Universal Energy desires my survival, my peace, my serenity. It is the same force that guides a fish to flow downstream of a mountainside.

The existence of a Higher Power need not be debated. The fact is that man played no part in this morning's sunrise. I am in awe of the powerful force responsible for such a feat. From the recognition of its existence comes my willingness to humbly accept that I, too, am a small fish flowing in the stream of life.

I trust in the inexplicable power that guides me. Today, the great challenge would be, not to believe.

In finding my Higher Power, I have found peace.

February 26

The Spirit Channel

There are two channels from which I receive inspiration. The mind channel was the first I had access to. Its programming choices are excess, confusion, doubt, resentment, jealousy, and fear. The program director is my delusional mind. The producer is my ego, always trying to protect me from any perceived threat to my character.

For a long time, this was the only channel from which programming was clear. During this time, I would run from one quick-fix bomb shelter to another to avoid the next incoming threat. There were times when I gave up, buried my head between my knees, and cried.

By some inexplicable miracle, on a bright sunny morning, with my head still throbbing from the previous night's bombing, I began to receive a signal from the Spirit Channel. At first, there was a lot of static. Over time, it became crystal clear. The programming is directed by my Inner Spiritual Instinct; the producer is my Higher Power. This channel offers clarity, faith, love, and hope.

Today, I have a choice. I can listen to the mind or the spirit. Programming from the mind results in chaos, while programming from the spirit results in peace.

February 27

A Spiritual Gift

I am responsible to share my gifts. These God-given life experiences include the happy times and the sad times, the obstacles and the solutions. Through my sharing, others know they are not alone.

At one time I felt terminally unique, that my experience was singular, that no one understood my greatest joys or my deepest hurts. Then one day, I was privy to hear someone share "their story," including how they overcame obstacles that I too was experiencing and for which I had no solution. I was touched and deeply affected by the message of hope.

"Their story" was "my story". By sharing our experiences, we not only help ourselves by giving voice to our hopes and hauntings, but also help others in their identification.

It is a two-way street of expression and reception. As we open our spirit to others, we allow them to open theirs to us. There is healing in our willingness to participate in open human interaction. In our sharing, we offer A Spiritual Gift.

February 28

Stoke The Fire of Recovery

It was an unhealthy relationship with self that opened the gates to addiction.

Chemical and behavioral mind altering initially brought relief to a defeated mind and tired soul, but quickly contributed to mental and moral chaos. To survive, I had to stop.

Not all desperate individuals find the miracle of recovery. For those of us who have inexplicably survived and experienced our moment of clarity, we must do the work to Stoke The Fire of Recovery, for if it goes out through procrastination or overconfidence, we will fall back into hell.

Healing involves finding a healthy acceptance of who we are and how we came to be. It requires a commitment to continued spiritual practice and the cultivation of inner peace. Only then can we live free from the grip of negativity and delusion.

Our ultimate goal is a life of serenity. To achieve this, we must stay stopped, develop healthy self-appreciation, and remain grateful for the miracle of clarity that ignites the roaring blaze of gratitude in our hearts.

February 29

Coming to Believe

I had a conversation with an individual who reported that he was stuck in his ability to Come to Believe in a "Higher Power." Although he has experienced many setbacks over the years, he has not given up on his ability to change. This is because he has witnessed the miracle of recovery in numerous others and knows that this may be the only process that offers a solution to his spiritual malady. To have even modest hope that this spiritual method might offer a way out of his dilemma is it not " Coming to Believe"?

The simplicity of this endeavor can easily confuse complicated, logical individuals seeking recovery. This is the "why" of how We can't do it alone. When We join together, We form a power greater than ourselves, a Higher Power.

With this simple, logical formula in hand, We begin to connect our mental capacity with our spiritual capacity.

This is the way We Come to Believe!

March 1

Lessons From The Past

The past is said to be gone, but it is not. It follows me wherever I go. The past cannot be erased; its memories are the footprints of my life. I sometimes experience periods of self-pity when I begin to think about the wreckage and missed opportunities of my yesteryears.

Over time, I have come to realize that there was little choice in the path I chose. I made the best decisions I could with the information I had at the time. The good, the bad, the indifferent, and the missed opportunities have all come together to make up the pieces of who I am today. It is in the fertile soil of this rich and sometimes turbulent history that the seeds of awareness, faith, and hope were sowed.

Memories of the past will continue to provide substance for healthy decision-making. But only if I surrender to the spiritual purpose of those lessons. Healthy detachment from the past lies in understanding that it does not define me, but also that I do not want to close the door on it.

There are still nuggets of gold to be mined in the treasured experiences of long ago.

March 2

The Gift Of Desperation

The Gift of Desperation has often been the source of motivation for my writing, meditating, or prayer. It has pushed me to become more involved in service and more open to sharing my thoughts and feelings with others. There is a knowledge that action transforms darkness into light.

It was The Gift of Desperation and a whisper from deep within that encouraged me to walk through the gates of recovery. The timing of the two had to be perfect for the miracle to happen. I was never to be the same again.

Twenty years into sobriety, I would receive this gift of desperation again. This time fueled not by substances but by deep emotional turmoil. Once again, I needed to take action. Action relieves the symptoms and heals the wound. Taking action could mean taking out my bow and arrows and lashing out or, taking action could mean going deeper in my meditation and prayer practices, increasing my service to others, and recommitting to taking better care of my physical self by eating right and exercising regularly.

By caring for my mind, body, and spirit, I became better equipped to face and accept my woundedness without firing the poisonous arrows of my hurt. Caring for my physical and spiritual self strengthened my connection to my Higher Power, resulting in a return of serenity.

There are times when the sun is hidden behind dark clouds. It is during these times that I allow the gift of desperation to guide me toward the light.

March 3

Living Humble

In today's society, it is commonly believed that the one with the most toys will be declared the winner. This leads to greed and self-centeredness, and there no humility in this way of living. Any attitude of superiority, conceit, or arrogance distances us from each other and from the Divine Power for Good in the World.

Unfortunately, it often takes great loss to develop gratitude for what we once had but did not value. Loss of health, material possessions, reputation, or a loved one can be the impetus that turns on the light of humility. In times of despair, we are driven closer to the light of Truth.

There are those who assume humility by performing humble acts, but does that define them as truly humble? When we can honestly say to ourselves that we would be willing to detach from all material possessions, justified anger, self-pity, and self-importance in order to live humbly as a trusted servant of Mother Earth, only then are we on our way to practicing humility.

To detach does not mean to get rid of. It means we do not allow possessions or negative character traits to influence our actions. We do not bow down to them or surrender to their power. We acknowledge their existence as part of our humanity, but we choose to live guided by the goodness of Spirit.

Practicing humility in all our affairs is the sure way to grow closer to each other and to the Spiritual Source.

March 4

I Was Humbled!

One day, through a series of unforeseen circumstances, in an instant, I lost financial security, found my character attacked, my name defamed, and all without recourse. I felt justified anger, injustice, self-pity, anxiety, and experienced many sleepless nights. I would either let this situation go or be dragged down by it. Act out or surrender. Feeling helpless, I turned to the only option available to me, prayer.

I was forced to detach from material security and self-importance. I asked my inner spiritual source to relieve me of any arrogance, pride, or grandiosity polluting my spirit. I worked through a natural resistance to humility and became grateful for what I still had. I became a trusted servant and accepted the guidance of The Unlimited Power of Wisdom and Love.

Finally, suddenly, unexpectedly, and without explanation, the cloud over my spirit lifted. There is still work to be done to recover what was robbed from my soul; some of the damage is beyond repair. However, I am truly grateful for the horrific experience because it gifted me increased humility, love, and appreciation.

I was humbled.

March 5

Purifying The Mind

Our real selves went into exile because of unacceptable shame, and we were left with our masked, superficial delusional selves. At the time, it appeared to those around us that we were absolutely self-centered, but in fact we were fighting for emotional survival through dysfunctional, destructive masquerading.

As a result of spiritual awakening, we come to accept ourselves as worthy and willing to embark on a journey of self-actualization. In the process, our true selves feel safe to reveal themselves once again. As we come to understand our troubled minds and begin to practice newfound humility and honesty, we let go of our shame and embrace that which has shamed us.

Ocean water was inadvertently unpurified by salt from the land and ocean floor, and so were our pure minds unpurified by delusional interpretations of life events.

Ocean water is purified by the process of desalination.

The mind is purified by the awakening of the spirit.

March 6

Healing Body and Mind

Physical discomfort is a signal from our body that something is not working as it should. We may tolerate the pain for a short time, but if it persists, we seek help. We are given a medical prescription that assures us that if we follow it, the discomfort will pass. We trust the help we have sought, we follow the instructions, and we heal.

Mental distress is the way our mind signals that we are practicing poor thinking. We may experience distress in the form of worry, fear, anger, resentment, shame, jealousy, or self-pity. If we accept these as natural to our human experience and accommodate dysfunctional coping skills, we will experience only temporary relief.

When we seek a spiritual solution with the same faith we brought to the medical remedy, we overcome our mental disturbances. It is by following spiritual guidance that we will heal our mental disruptions and come to know peace.

March 7

Show Up For Life

There are mornings when my delirious mind awakens before my spiritual inner self. By the time I am fully conscious, it has planned my day and often traveled far into the future. This triggers fears and insecurities about the unknown and my ability to fulfill my responsibilities. Rarely is there any real validity to these delusions.

There have been mornings when I've pulled the covers over my head and let fear win. To overcome fear, I plant my feet on the ground and Show Up For Life. I challenge delusional thoughts by becoming spiritually centered and bringing myself into the present moment. Delusions exist only in the future. In the now, they lose all power.

Once present, I can show up for any of life's many challenges with the confidence that I am good enough and have the capacity to perform at the level that the Divine Power for Good has intended for me.

I am only responsible for the effort, not the outcome!

March 8

The Spiritual Source

From the beginning, the human species has developed a belief in a power greater than itself. All civilizations including the Greeks, the Romans, the Incas, the great African tribes, the Buddhists, the Christians, the Jews, the Muslims, have accepted the guidance of a great power that influenced the way they approached their lives, their destiny, and their afterlife.

We come to believe or not to believe, to worship, to fear, or to ignore this omnipotent power. Even non-believers, in times of great crisis, must wonder, if only for a moment, if there might be divine intervention.

On a daily basis, I choose to enrich my relationship with the Spiritual Source. In doing so, I feel more connected to the planet, to my inner being, and to all the individuals I encounter on this journey.

We can choose to live under the influence of our delusional mind or accept the guidance of our Inner Survival Instinct.

March 9

A Simple Life

Living a life of simplicity is a concept that challenges modern day thinking.

Our distant ancestors were concerned with survival above all else. They needed only the bare essentials—air, shelter, love, food, and water—to live. No individual was driven to accumulate more than another, for such desires held no purpose. They lived in harmony with one another, let only by the Natural Order of the Universe.

Despite our so-called evolution, we could still survive on the same basic needs. Yet, our modern pursuit has shifted toward material accumulation. This constant desire to keep up with our neighbor, breeds insecurity and restlessness. We have become consumed by the need to plan for an uncertain future, driven not by necessity, but by fear and greed.

We would do well to return to our humble beginnings. Through gratitude and a deep appreciation for the precious gift of today, we may once again find our way to a Simple Life.

March 10

Aligning Our Will

When we align our will with that of the Divine Source, we will live the destiny intended for us.

How do we go about knowing the Will of the Universe for us? To get to that answer, we must develop a Spiritual Practice. Let us agree at the outset that there is no certainty that we will ever know an intended will with certainty. The importance of the spiritual quest is that it enriches our daily journey, not that it anticipates a destination.

We surrender to the Spirit's Will for us by allowing ourselves to flow without struggle down the river of life. We allow our personal Spiritual Guide to guide us on our journey. We accept our path, making only slight adjustments to avoid treacherous obstacles.

The river of life is not without its cascades and waterfalls. Our struggles are the result of our choices. To overcome them, we let go of rigidity and fear, and trust our Guide. It's in trying to avoid the inevitable that we find our difficulties.

Rivers flow with ease from source to delta. By aligning our will with that of the Divine Source, we too, will find our intended destination as we travel this eternal mystery.

March 11

Living By Moral Principles

We may never know the purpose of the events of our lives or their true meaning. We don't know if life is predestined or a random act. This remains a great mystery to us all. Regardless of the many unanswered questions about our human experience, there are principles that have been established over thousands of years that can guide us toward a more meaningful life.

I fear that the morals of our world have become irreversibly corrupt. We seem to be drifting further apart. Individually, there may be little we can do to bring about global change, but to bring the glory of the Master into our daily actions. In this way we can influence those who share our path.

By living by the moral principles of integrity, loyalty, compassion, equality, and purity, we will radiate a righteous aura to all who enter our spiritual field. Our humble spiritual energy will ripple out to those around us, softening their day. They in turn will ripple out to those they touch.

In this way, we do our part to bring about what we want to see in the world.

March 12

We Are Worthy

Before we were in recovery, our lives were filled with disappointment and hurt. When we look back at the wreckage of the past, we can see that it was filled with chaotic behavior, guided only by destructive thinking. When the miracle happens, our thoughts begin to reflect our new state of mind and new way of being.

Once back on the path to our intended destination, we must choose to think, work, and expect only the best for ourselves, for We Are Worthy. We may have strayed from the divine path, but we can now see that only there would we encounter the hard lessons for our growth. It was hard to live off the spiritual grid. It took great courage to survive such conditions and to rise again. Rather than wallow in the sorrow of our past, we dedicate our lives to working for the good of our future.

Our best may not always be recognized by others or rewarded by society's reward system. We do not seek recognition, but inner resolution. Our Divine Source is the only judge of our best, we should seek His guidance on our journey for in His eyes We Are Worthy.

March 13

Envy

We often compare our worth to that of our neighbors. The size of our house, car, bank account, paycheck, appearance, family, or happiness can be units of comparison. This leads to unwanted envy.

Envy eats away at us and interferes with how we relate to others and ourselves. It denies us the joy of recognizing our accomplishments and gets in the way of praising others, thus depriving their self-worth of nourishment.

I wish to be free of envy and commit myself to praise rather than compare. By enthusiastically praising the success of others, I will lift them and myself to greater spiritual heights.

March 14

Anonymity and Gratitude

The "mistakes" of yesterday were misguided attempts to find illusory happiness. Guided only by self-will, I sought immediate gratification and reward in a game of fame and fortune.

There wasn't enough attention to satisfy my underlying low self-esteem. I developed an addiction to people-pleasing for self-reward. There weren't enough gains to satisfy the need for attention and approval.

I blindly sought acceptance and love, but my methods were doomed to disappointment. I looked outward, unaware that the happiness I sought was an inside job.

Once learned from, the "mistakes" of the past became invaluable guides to accomplishment in the future. That future is today, and the accomplishment is the humility to move forward by accepting the righteous guidance of the Great Spirit. With such guidance, I live happily and anonymously grateful.

March 15

A Genuine Smile

The joyful expression of a genuine smile is the most precious gift we can give to the universe. It conveys our peaceful openness to join another in a unique, precious moment.

Smiling releases feel-good chemicals in our brains. It lifts our mood, relaxes our body, and brings joy to those around us. Anyone can smile, but a genuine smile offers more than a facial expression, for its deep energy erupts from our loving soul.

Our joyful expression is naturally ignited when we embrace an honest desire to be of service to all individuals. When we are serene and completely at the mercy of our Spiritual Guide, all darkness leaves our Being and our contagious smile causes a ripple effect of joy in the universe.

March 16

It Takes A Village

We should all have people in our lives we turn to for guidance—individuals who have traveled the road we're on and triumphed over the challenges we face. In addition to these, we will encounter many other teachers along the way.

All people and situations are placed in our path with perfect timing. Accepting this, we will look for the good in all the people we meet and experiences we have. We will welcome them into our lives. If we live the alternative, we use judgment to discard some as without merit or purpose. Dismissing the lesson they were sent to teach can be a serious mistake.

It Takes a Village to lift us over life's obstacles. All people, moments, and experiences have meaning, regardless of their packaging. By accepting all as our teachers, we show gratitude and respect for their intended purpose.

There are no coincidences, all interactions and experiences have a spiritual meaning.

March 17

A Wise Man or Woman

A wise man or woman is one who, in times of adversity, allows their calmness to rise to the occasion. Developing a state of calm is a prerequisite for a serene life.

We will face seemingly insurmountable challenges in our lifetime. These may include health concerns, financial insecurity, relationship hurts, and many others. How are we to remain tranquil during these challenging times? The primary emotional response to them is hardly controllable.

When adversity visits, we allow it space to vent. Ignoring it feeds its power. Instead of fighting it with resistance, which deepens our difficulties and darkens our spirit, we slowly detach from torment by embracing inner calm and thus prevent it from consuming us.

To develop a state of calm, we strive to practice the spiritual principles of acceptance and tolerance. With the help of our spiritual guide and his forward-looking eye, our calmness grows, and serenity arrives. This is the path of the wise woman or man.

March 18

Natural and Spiritual Laws

Natural laws are easy to understand; our lives have a beginning and an end. Human experience presents us with successes and failures, happiness, and sorrow. We overcome some challenges and are baffled by others. We feel exuberant love and debilitating pain. Natural laws are limited.

Spiritual laws exist to interpret human suffering. Spirit is called upon for guidance when our acceptance of natural laws fails us. Our human shortcomings are overcome through spiritual practice. Spiritual laws offer limitless insight.

Natural laws and spiritual laws can dance as one once we master the understanding and acceptance that life's discomforts exist as part of our human existence.

Our human experience is the university that the spirit attends to become enlightened.

March 19

Searching for Happiness

If the goal of life is to experience happiness, then how do we go about finding this elusive and often seemingly unattainable state of mind?

Fleeting happiness can be experienced as a result of achieving goals, casual relationships, or material accumulation. True, lasting happiness appears as a by-product of the way we live. It's not a result of accomplishments, people, or material possessions.

Seeking a path to lasting happiness in no way excludes our desire to achieve goals, our yearning for a loving relationship, or for our want for amenities that bring us comfort. Ultimately, it's not what we have, but how we went about getting it, and how we go about sharing it.

Happiness is the end result of living selflessly. The way to harness this most precious gift is to find a balance between our yearnings, wants, and desires and in our practice of humility and altruism.

March 20

The Cues

Life is not a series of random events. Not a predictable routine to be followed in a linear direction. If it were, we would only experience the conscious mind. We'd dot the i's, cross the t's, and end our journey satisfied that we'd gotten all we could out of this earthly experience.

If we were to develop awareness of the messages that the Divine Universe sends us in the form of life events or inspirational moments, we might be tempted to follow those cues. We would want to take a risk and follow the light that cuts through the gray shadows and monotony of our days. It takes courage to leave the familiar and move toward the spiritually unseen.

We must accept that we are more than our bodies and minds. Within us exists a Survival Spirit that receives subtle cues, gentle urgings in the form of Divine Inspiration, meant to guide us, toward the path of self-actualization.

If we follow the cues, we will be brought to our uniquely intended place of purpose in this human experience.

March 21

The Chief Advisor

The mind is advised by the ego, which is by nature self-centered and ignorant of all but itself. Often the mind becomes so overwhelmed that it surrenders control to the influence of the ego. This leads to selfish decisions whose sole purpose is for the ego to beat its chest. There is no humility in the ego. Winning at all costs is its creed. A life lived in this way is devoid of empathy or compassion.

If we develop a strong principled spirit, which, like a muscle, needs daily exercise to strengthen, then our mind has been presented with a second option for an advisor. This one is wiser, gentler, and more humble in its approach. The spirit can calm the mind so that it becomes focused and reasonable. The Spirit provides a refuge for principled decision making.

The tyrant ego can only be quieted by the light of the spirit. If we are to live a principled life, we must allow Spirit, not Ego, to be our mind's Chief Advisor.

March 22

Mind Heart Spirit

Our choices are guided by one of three sources: the Mind, the Heart, or the Spirit.

The mind seeks pleasure and the avoidance of all suffering. It makes clear choices of all or nothing. When it senses a positive outcome, it pushes us forward, but when there is doubt, it holds us back.

The heart, filled with passion, romanticizes all imaginable desires. It does not use logic to lead us to a supposed outcome.

Spirit rises above pleasure and suffering, passion and outcome, and brings our awareness to Truth. Spirit provides balance between the mind and the heart.

Fantasy is more appealing than reality. Perhaps that is why we find it hard to Believe. It is only by seeking the Truth that we come to know of Spirit.

March 23

A River's Flow

Rivers surrender to their journey; they are aligned with the will of the universe, guided by Universal Intelligence. They flow freely from the source to delta without a struggle.

An Omnipotent Force directs all living organisms and is responsible for the perfect order of our world. We too, are part of this perfect order, but our willful minds rebel against the natural order of existence.

Instead of allowing ourselves to flow from birth to eternal rest, we live lives of unnecessary conflict. We ignore the guidance of Universal Intelligence and choose the direction of a delusional mind, the sole cause of all our human struggles.

In possession of the undeniable Truth that this is a unique human experience from which we seek only pure joy, why do we allow ourselves so much struggle and suffering? We struggle because we don't want to give up even part of our self-will or control.

In order to minimize our human suffering we ought to strive for less dependence on the mind and seek to align our will with that of Universal Intelligence.

March 24

Spirit Consciousness

Prayer is the tool we use to engage Spirit Consciousness and move from delusional thinking to spiritual awareness.

When we are in a state of delusion, it is as if we are in the eye of a hurricane. We see no way out and only horrible scenarios surround us. We become trapped in our current crisis.

Prayer brings a spiritual perspective to overwhelming situations. In prayer, we detach from the chaos. We step out of the eye of the hurricane and can better predict the direction of the storm, receive spiritual guidance, and avoid mayhem.

Prayer may not always provide the solution we seek. At the very least, it allows us momentary calm. In the gap between thought and action, we let go of delusional outcomes and place our concerns in the divine hands of the Eternal Heart.

Prayer is the way out of destabilizing delusion and a path to empowerment through Spirit Consciousness.

March 25

Outgrowing Innocence

Once we outgrow the innocence of our childhood years, we begin to encounter the delusional expectations of life. We outgrow the excitement of the first day of school and instead experience the uncertainty and dread of the first day at a new job. The anticipation of the first day of summer vacation turns into the hasty planning of a weekend getaway. The joy of the holidays becomes the financial burden of gift-giving. The warm anticipation of family gatherings is replaced by the purposeful avoidance of a resentful past.

In our younger years, we were free from judgment, resentment, shame, and fear. How then did we shift and allow negative emotions to undermine our serenity?

Negative emotions arise from our inability to live up to society's unwritten expectations. When we compare ourselves to others or feel that we don't measure up, we feel inadequate.

When we let go of trying to meet the delusional expectations of human-doing and replace them with the ease of human-being, we encounter the freedom and innocence of long ago.

By once again being free to be me, I discovered my serenity.

March 26

Consciousness of Spirit

Consciousness of Spirit is a profound awareness of a Higher Power. Although the attainment of enlightenment is reserved for those who devote their entire being to absolute union with a God of their understanding, we too can taste this sweet nectar.

The rewards of the material realm cannot satisfy our insatiable desire for material well-being. Shortly after experiencing a fleeting moment of joy; the new job, promotion, car, partner, vacation, or house, we are filled with desire for the next fix. It takes tireless effort to experience fleeting moments of happiness, and we are never fully satisfied.

We begin to experience Consciousness of Spirit the moment we make a sincere effort to commune with a Higher Power, for we will have begun to detach from our worldly anchors.

Things of the spirit challenge a mind conditioned by the material world. It takes dedication, consistency, and sacrifice to maintain Consciousness of Spirit.

Should we remain on the spiritual path, we will come to know that we already possess the greatest gift of all; that of being a spiritual being given the opportunity to have this unique human experience.

March 27

Journey of Recovery

We are born with purity of heart. We are Children of the Great Thinker. We do not choose our family, our environment, or the culture into which we are born. Initially, all decisions are made for us. We have few choices. We become willing participants in the dramas of life.

Healing is the process of re-establishing a loving relationship with our inner child that was lost somewhere back when we were unconsciously guided by external forces. Once we become aware of the wounding that our past has inflicted upon us, we can change direction and choose the process of healing or recovery. We can begin to take care of ourselves by shedding the many layers of resentment, shame, disappointment and guilt. We change direction by changing our purpose in life.

The focus of our daily purpose is to become a blessing in the life of another. We attract goodness by spreading goodness. We experience the gifts of this new way of living, and we will want more. Others will sense that our lives have new happiness and meaning. They too will want to live this way. In this way, a hurting and empty individual can not only change his or her direction but, by living purposefully, can have an immeasurable impact on the lives of others.

This slow, and miraculous process is the Journey of Recovery.

The Journey of Recovery

March 28

Criticism

Criticism is a form of judgment, which is an unaffordable luxury.

Self-encouragement rather than self-criticism validates our accomplishments, no matter how small. It is crucial to move away from doubt and harsh reflection and replace them with congratulatory validation of our efforts. After all, we are only responsible for the effort, not the outcome.

This in no way excuses us from responsibility for the choices we make and the impact they have on our lives and the lives of others. We are to be honest with ourselves at all times, yet refrain from emotional punishment. Failure is a lesson that motivates change and prepares us for future success.

Our criticism of others is self-centered because we are selfishly trying to increase our own self-worth. We must be aware that criticism hurts and often humiliates others. Instead of being cynical critics, we should guide and support our coworkers, friends, and family members. We should look only for the good in others, and in this way we will see the good in ourselves.

Criticism whether spoken or silent, whether directed at ourselves or others, has no place in a peaceful heart.

March 29

The VIP Invitation

At the root of my dysfunction was low self-worth. Hiding in my subconscious, out of reach of my conscious mind, it would become fertile ground for a spiritual malady to flourish. In a world where success is rewarded with a VIP invitation to the imperial ball, I was a mere spectator watching the chosen ones being escorted through the golden gates.

Along came mind-altering substances and behaviors; they fed my insecurities a dose of grandiosity, and I was transformed into a lord. The feeling of superiority did not last. In short order, the addiction reclaimed its magic. It had preyed on my low self-worth. It gave me a false sense of security and grandeur. By the time it spit me out, I had become a useless court jester.

Both inferiority and superiority are but mental deceptions. Reality lies in the spiritual understanding that as children of the same Spiritual Source, our worth is in our deeds.

Search deep within yourself. Hidden behind your pride, fear, or insecurities, you will find a golden envelope with your VIP invitation to a celebration of love and equality at the home of the Great Spirit of the Universe.

March 30

Breaking the Trance

My relationship with mind-altering substances and compulsive behaviors became toxic. My mind was poisoned, as evidenced by my delusional thinking, and increased conflict with self, others, and the world.

I was in a trance, devoid of any sense of reality.

Breaking the Trance came about by experiencing a moment of grace granted by the Good Shepherd. I was restored to sanity. But not all at once!

I am vigilant against temptation's seductive call. I do not fear it; I respect it. In its wake I play the tape through. The end is always the same, a return to the insanity of my former ways. I have evidenced in others that with each relapse, their bottom grows deeper.

My most cherished relationship is with my Spiritual Guide, who has graciously guided me to clear thinking and a loving soul. Since Breaking the Trance, I have made a daily choice to accept reality, from which there is no plausible escape.

March 31

Do Not Fight Back

Our first reaction to being hurt is to fight back.

When we become punitive in thought or action toward another, our retaliation feeds our anger and creates resentment. Vindictiveness brings inner turmoil, and in this way, we taint our loving hearts and unsettle our spirit.

What hurts one person may pass unnoticed by another. This Truth reminds us that pain does not arise solely from the event, but from the way we internalize it.

Though the hurt feels real, and it is, its roots are often found within our own perceptions, our beliefs, our past experiences. To heal, we must look inward with compassion, recognizing that our spirit is not wounded by the circumstance, but by the meaning we give to it.

We Do Not Fight Back; instead, we de-escalate our sentiment, and with a mind and heart of forgiveness, we purge our intent of malice and seek calm.

This is the foundation of a life of compassion. It may go against earthly instinct, but it's the only solution if we are to experience peace on our human journey.

April 1

The Biggest Lie Ever Told

The Biggest Lie Ever Told is that we are self-sufficient. In moments of euphoria, when we feel autonomous, grandiosity quietly strips away humility.

Flaunting our great assets, whether material or social, gives us a false sense of superiority, blinding us to the Truth that true worth is not measured by what we possess, but by who we really are.

We may think others are jealous of our position, but only those suffering from the same malady of the spirit will envy our lifestyle.

Materialism has an insatiable appetite that cannot be satisfied. We cannot praise a false god and expect real love. If we think ourselves superior, we will find loneliness.

Alone and self-oriented, we may accumulate objects, but never enough to satisfy our ravenous appetite. The value of evolving a God of our understanding is such, that the temple of our soul will overflow with endless love.

April 2

Hitting Bottom

Hitting Bottom was the experience of complete ego deflation; total loss of self and purpose. It was looking in the mirror and seeing the hopelessness etched in my eyes and not recognizing who I had become. It was the awareness that my life had lost direction or purpose. Hitting Bottom was my spirit's calling, imploring me that something was amiss-that I was dying inside.

I had become helpless in the face of circumstances. Although I had felt this discomfort for some time, on this particular day, I honestly admitted my inability to overcome my pain alone.

The Spirit sent up another flair.

This time, I followed His lead.

April 3

New Freedom and Happiness

When we come to accept our spiritual malady as the source for our addiction, depression, or compulsive behaviors, without the burden of guilt or blame, we will have received the key that opens the door to recovery.

The leap of faith over this threshold is challenging, for we have long since lost hope. The sober chapter of our lives is just around the corner. If we do not quit before the miracle happens, we will experience freedom from compulsion, anxiety, victimization, fear, and self-pity.

For those of us that chanced faith and walked toward the light emanating from our Truth, we discovered a New Freedom and Happiness that embraced us with inner spiritual tranquility and peace toward the world.

April 4

Return To Sanity

A faint glow of light appeared at the far end of what seemed to be an endless dark tunnel of madness. To return to sanity, we had no other choice but to walk toward it.

Once we learn of salvation, savage thinking is threatened. Our spirit will have found a crack through which a glimmer of hope enters our lives and challenges doubt and despair. We will come to believe that there is another way. For a disturbed mind, the choice is still unclear. Having been conditioned to darkness, we wonder if we can again live in the light.

The glimmer of hope awakened our spiritual curiosity. That which we doubted, now has a plausible solution. Coming to believe is the starting point for a return to sanity and the journey of spiritual healing.

April 5

A Door to The Past

Our past holds regrets for not having fulfilled our expectations, however delusional they may have been. For these we need not apologize, for we will come to know that they have contributed to the discovery of our spiritual purpose. That same past also contains resilience, survival, and even achievements that, however insignificant we may think them, have value.

For the hurt we have caused, we sincerely ask forgiveness and make amends wherever possible. Today we will love twice as hard, double our compassion and dedicate ourselves to being of service.

We use our perceived failures and costly lessons as a solid foundation on which to build our new way of being. Inspired by the grace of a new life, we go forth to do our spiritual bidding, mindful not to shut the door on our past.

April 6

Giving Up Control.

As the captain of my ship, I was ill-prepared to read a chart or follow the direction of a compass and fell into dangerous seas. Chaos distracted me from my moral boundaries, making my spiritual death feel inevitable. Without rescue, I would have drowned.

The moment of truth came, and with no logical solution, I handed over the helm to the Master of Sea and Land. It was meant to be temporary, for I fully intended to regain control. In a short time, I came to appreciate the simplicity of being a mere passenger. The Master navigated my life gracefully over smooth seas and danced with turbulence.

On the occasions when I insist on taking back control, I experience again the unpleasantness of fear and doubt. Every day he renews his offer to guide my life.

I think I'll let him!

April 7

Know of Serenity

We come to know serenity as the simplicity of well-being. No matter what circumstances or emotions we are experiencing, there is calm beneath the surface. This tranquility is only possible because we've adapted to a way of life in which we've accepted the guidance of the Master of Unlimited Power, Wisdom, and Love.

We've given up willful expectation and surrendered our misguided will to Him. We have stopped labeling situations as good or bad and no longer ask, "Why is this happening to me?" Instead, we ponder, "What do you want me to learn from this, Father?

Recovery seeks to eliminate the rollercoaster of life. It guides us to discover our emotional equilibrium, a neutral place somewhere between human doing and human being. By living in the moment and detaching from an outcome, we come to Know of Serenity.

April 8

Honesty and Humility

Being of clear mind, I relinquished control and accepted guidance from a Higher Power. I then set about investigating the details of my past. The inventory revealed the components that contributed to my dis-ease and the damage caused by my reckless addiction.

My foggy recollection cleared as I methodically reviewed my history. Conscious awareness of the impact the malady had on so many innocent others caused extreme sorrow, shame, and self-judgment. As I continued inventory, I emotionally detached from the events, as if the watcher, narrating a story. After all, I was not the same person. I had changed. I'd renewed myself to a new way of being.

I received assurance that by being thorough I was taking the first steps toward Honesty and Humility. This exercise demanded honest scrutiny of character for it was from this foundation that I would go about moral reparation.

April 9

Know Peace

We do not know peace because we have become accustomed to anger, worry, sorrow, and disappointment. We waste precious time trying to recover by chasing after happiness.

We believe that happiness comes from external conditions, even though we know and say it isn't so. Yet, material well-being attracts us as a source of comfort.

Inner Peace is the only true source of lasting happiness. We find this Peace by turning inward through periods of quiet inner reflection and meditation. As we strive to quiet our minds, we experience distance from earthly things and draw closer to spirit-inspired Truths.

If we persevere in a life guided by the Spirit, we will come to Know Peace.

April 10

Liberating Confession

The survey of my reckless life caused me grief, shame and self-judgment—consuming me for a time. I found freedom from self-pity through confession.

I shared my inventory with another and the heavy burden of guilt lifted. I was surprised that my confidant expressed identification with my experiences. My uniqueness had been a myth all along.

Words provide a mental sketch of reality, but lack spiritual substance. To liberate what I found unexplainable or indescribable with words, I had to engage my soul. In the silence of my mind, I offered the same inventory to a Higher Power.

Guided by Spirit, I allowed the purity of Truth to rise from the depths of my being. I accepted before myself and the God of my understanding of the exact nature of my wrongs, free from deception or justification.

While we might be tempted to sway our Truth before others, to do so before God is to alter little of our character. Liberating Confession frees us from the bondage of self.

April 11

Benefiting others

A spiritual malady is a virus of the mind. It is a state of being guided by an ego running scared of ill-constructed thoughts of doubt and fragility. It is a treacherous viper, its tail rattling, its fangs outstretched, ready to strike at anything threatening the ego's survival. And yet this vicious snake is easily calmed by the soothing sounds of the snake charmer's flute. Our charmers; spirit and our support group, work in mysterious ways to tame our compulsions and in leading us toward healing.

Once recovered from our obsessions, we ask ourselves, "Why was I spared?" Or, "What was the purpose of my pain?" The next time a broken spirit crosses our path seeking relief, we have our answer. Our experiences help them know recovery exists, for only one sufferer can truly empathize with another.

In this way, no matter how far down the ladder we may have gone, we know a Higher Power spared us for the benefit of others.

April 12

Pursuit of Righteousness

A thorough inventory and a liberating confession made me aware of my wrongful conduct. By taking responsibility for my wrongdoings, I undertook a moral cleansing.

I immediately examined the character flaws that had become apparent in my story. While I shudder at my past self and behavior, I address them by confronting and accepting my imperfections, coupled with a strong desire to improve.

These false protectors of ego and delusion serve no purpose in a life of sobriety. Their removal allows me to lift my head and meet the eyes of others without fear, for I walk in the honest Pursuit of Righteousness.

April 13

Usefulness and Gratitude

I fell into a predictable negative pattern of life, devoid of all things Spirit.

My joy came from external factors. My world shrank. I became of service to none but myself. The feeling of uselessness washed away my ambition. Disillusionment and self-pity opened the door to dysfunction.

Once on the healing path, Spirit filled me with faith, and I found purpose. Initially, by helping a newcomer who arrived at the gateway of recovery, battered and confused, by sharing my experiences and allowing for them to find identification.

Eventually, the Light of Spirit guided me to a life of service to a diverse group of people. I risked a new way of being, and in so doing, my dysfunction became usefulness, my self-pity became gratitude.

April 14

A Well-Groomed Garden

If left unattended, character defects become quite visible to all, like unwelcome weeds in a well-tended botanical garden. Only through constant vigilance and daily uprooting can the observant gardener keep his garden free of them.

We are powerless over our negative traits but can manage their threat with continued awareness and effort.

It is by accepting inner spiritual guidance, decreasing pride and increasing humility that we will begin to reduce the resurgence of our meddlesome traits and our character will become like the gardener's well-tended botanical garden.

April 15   The Journey of Recovery

Taking Interest in Others

This business of prioritizing others challenges the theory that we must place on our oxygen mask first. It's important not to interpret such an expression literally, but instead to draw inspiration from the deeper message it aims to convey.

When we live guided by our innermost compassionate self, we naturally find a balance between caring for ourselves and being mindful of others.

When in doubt, begin by caring for someone else. Consider how your actions might impact their well-being. While selfishness can offer fleeting satisfaction, our past self-centered behaviors are reminders of the chaos they once created. Prioritizing the needs of others is how we begin to live beyond the boundaries of self-centeredness.

Spiritual awareness of our fellow human beings gives way to living in peace and harmony with all.

April 16

Taking Responsibility

Through acceptance and forgiveness, we repair our relationship with ourselves, but we won't fully transform into a new way of being until we take full responsibility for the harmful actions done to others.

We retire to a quiet place and list those whom our self-centered behavior has caused worry, betrayal, or disrespect. We strive to be thorough, and though some may escape our present remembrance, it will certainly not be out of convenience.

We generate compassion for everyone on our list and ask our Higher Power to relieve them of our wrongdoing. We also ask that our guilt and shame be eased. Then, knowing the harm cannot be undone, we silently pray for spiritual understanding and forgiveness.

This process diminishes our guilt for the malice we caused by our actions and allows us to acknowledge our wrongs to those we have harmed. When we're ready, we begin the process of reparation.

April 17

Our Charitable Heart

The quest to satisfy our material and personal needs is a daily concern, for without food, shelter, and love, we have little chance of survival. Since this is the basis of survival for the entire human race, it carries a heavy responsibility, for we must share these vital elements with others.

Self-seekers have become proficient in accumulating goods and power but have lost their sensitivity to others. They too can recover!

When we live guided by the spirit, as we meet our human needs, we are reminded that not everyone is bountiful. We open our charitable heart, and in doing so, self-seeking slips away.

April 18

Reparation

Self-growth involves a thorough initial inventory of our past. Whether our malady is chemical, emotional, or behavioral, we must identify when our actions have caused harm and make amends.

Reparation happens by humbly approaching each person on our list, whenever possible, and without reservation or expectation, to acknowledge our wrong before them by word or deed.

We will look some in the eye. Where our contact would prove disruptive to another's life and, therefore, be self-serving, we ask forgiveness through contemplation and prayer.

Yet, our responsibility doesn't end there. It requires consistent unraveling and inquiry. Be it a week or ten years later, we remain responsible for making amends to those we may have left off our original list.

Amidst this process, and "before we are halfway through," the doors of spiritual clarity and insight open, for we have shown a commitment to "go to any length" to take responsibility for our harmful actions.

April 19

Attitude and Outlook

Negative attitudes and outlooks arise when we become trapped in negative thinking. They isolate us from aspiration and stifle commitment. Once we believe, we cannot un-believe. Belief makes all things possible.

The moment we accept the slightest possibility of a Higher Power, we inhale our first breath of hope and begin our journey toward spiritual healing. This breath, this possibility, is a beam of light that pierces our dark world.

Inspired by our newfound freedom from a disease of the mind and guided by the Power of All Possibility, we move forward in our new life. Transformed by the power of Spirit, fellowship and purpose, we experience a new Attitude and Outlook on life.

April 20

Daily Inventory

We begin each morning by asking our Higher Power for guidance and courage to help us live His Will, we align ourselves with this intention throughout the day. At night, when we engage in communion with HP, we can review our progress and express our gratitude for the lessons we've learned.

When we suddenly feel emotional or physical discomfort, it's often a message from our inner guide signaling that something needs attention. By pausing to reflect, we can uncover the source, shed light on it, and restore balance. Taking gentle inventory of our thoughts and feelings throughout the day helps prevent dis-ease and protects our inner peace.

By monitoring our thoughts, feelings, actions, and intentions, we are better equipped to stay true to living by spiritual principles and less likely to allow our defects to hinder our spiritual progress. Our inquiry brings awareness to obstacles to our growth and exposes hidden flaws.

Through honest self-evaluation, we gain insight into the necessary changes that remain. With a loving heart, we ask our Higher Power to remove these so that we can be of valuable service to our kindred spirits.

April 21

Underlying Fear

For years, I heard others speak of an underlying fear that they claimed was at the root of their spiritual malady. Fear of people, economic insecurity, or physical health robs us of optimism and unsettles our serenity. At that time, I could not identify fear in my life. I was living undisturbed. But fear was always there. It's a primal human emotion.

When turbulence hit my life, fear erupted like a volcano, its thick smoke swallowing all other emotions. I suddenly came face to face with this powerful force sitting quietly just below the surface of my consciousness. I had to spend time and effort stabilizing my spiritual foundation because I hadn't built it to withstand such catastrophic circumstances.

In the process of strengthening my spiritual footing, my relationship with my Spiritual Guide grew, for it is only by seeking to know His Will for me that I avoid disaster. The dark cloud of fear gave way to rich spiritual understanding.

Faith replaced fear.

April 22

Prayer and Meditation

Only through pain did I become willing to explore, believe, and depend on the Divine Consciousness of the Universe. The greater the pain, the greater the need to place my life situations in the Divine Hands that soothe my emotions, calm my thoughts, and lift my spirit.

Through continuous conscious and disciplined devotion to seeking guidance, I found the solution to overcoming obstacles that stand in the way of my inner peace. I access this through the process of Prayer and Meditation. In prayer, I bring focused awareness to my earthly limitations. In meditation, I receive the spiritual answer.

As with all skills, developing and maintaining conscious contact with a God of my understanding takes time, practice, and commitment.

Only in this way do I experience lasting inner peace.

April 23

Overcoming Challenges

All living organisms rely on instinct for survival. Although there is no physical evidence for a Higher Power's existence, it is an understandable concept.

Could Universal Intelligence be guiding nature's instincts—like a brook flowing into a mountain stream or the sunrise after a starry night?

Could spiritual consciousness guide human instincts? If so, is it acceptable that a spiritual survival instinct guides our lives?

When we become open to the power of Spirit and move to consciously welcome it into our lives, we begin to experience Spirit Conscious; we gain awareness of an uncomplicated way of living; as natural as the flight of a bird and as peaceful as the setting sun of a lazy afternoon. In the process, we acquire a previously unavailable intuition that lifts us over challenges that in the past have baffled us.

April 24

Carry the Message

As a result of the effort we put into our spiritual journey, we reach a peak of spiritual understanding—a magnificent view reserved for those who become willing to muddle through their various states of confusion.

From spiritual heights, we will awaken to see what cannot be unseen. The experience will have changed us, and we will have accumulated spiritual knowledge. With this comes responsibility, for we cannot keep it unless we give it away.

Our Higher Power requests we model these liberating principles so that others may know of the presence of a loving spirit and decide for themselves to accept and live by His guidance. For if not for us, who will tell of such an existence?

It is our calling to carry the message. We don't preach, lecture, or try to convince. We simply share our story when guided by Spirit or logic. We are reminded of our own resistance and the delicate way we came to believe.

In sharing what we deeply cherish, our spiritual bounty will grow plentiful.

April 25

Go With the Flow

All the little "coincidences" in my life have a purpose. When I am aligned with The Divine Consciousness of the Universe, I come to understand their intentions. Some are clear in the moment, others I become aware of, years later as missed opportunities.

I often do not know how to overcome an unbearable moment or situation, and suddenly, unexpectedly, the solution manifests itself without my effort. These unplanned or unimaginable little miracles led me to accept the existence of a Guiding Spirit. Today, it is very clear that these were not mere coincidences.

If I have to exert myself, I am probably forcing my will and ignoring the Will of the Universe. I am straining against Spirit Nature. We have the option of resisting guidance and rowing upstream with all our might, or we can accept direction and allow our life to Go With the Flow to its intended destination.

Following the Will of the Universe is best understood by actively seeking and practicing spiritual Truth. If we choose to live in this way, we will soon know Spirit is doing for us what we could not do through our will alone.

April 26

Another Angel Got His Wings

Addiction is a tsunami of the mind. It destroys everything in its path and drowns out all reason or logic. For many, the spiritual path is the only option keeping them from being swallowed by the ocean of addiction.

Many suffering from this disease receive introduction in recovery principles. They seem relieved that there is a solution to their perplexing lives, but never fully accept spirituality as an integral part of their process.

The relentlessness of addiction does not allow for their surrender. There are those whose dis-eased minds do not open to the power of Spirit to cut the shackles of addiction. Many lose the battle, leaving behind confused, grieving, loving families with so many unanswered questions.

Addiction poisons the mind, body, and soul. An antidote is spiritual conversion. Desperation, devotion, and commitment become catalyzers for surrender, spiritual guidance, and a complete transformation.

To those blessed with recovery, it is likely that you have benefited from the help of others in finding your peace. Celebrate your freedom and show gratitude for your favor by allowing the loving spirit to guide you to extend your hand to another who is struggling.

Being a blessing in the life of another is how we pay homage to those we have lost, and honor those who have paved the way for the miracle of recovery in our lives.

April 27

Bring About Goodness

Our outlook determines our mood. Our mood determines how we interpret the world and how we interact with ourselves and others.

Given our daily exposure to human and environmental injustice, a pessimistic outlook on the world is plausible. As a society, we have become a mirror of what we see around us. To protect our faith and lack of trust in humanity, and our emotional well-being from discouragement, we've erected barriers.

To dispel evil, we will establish a spiritual relationship with the Creator of Love and bring about goodness. We do not have to wait for the world to change. Through our human spirit, we can be the spark that illuminates the surrounding darkness.

Spiritual well-being brings a positive outlook and a kind disposition. With faith, we keep the eternal flame of hope lit, to guide us as we collaborate with like-minded others to bring about the change the world desperately needs.

April 28

Indispensable Human Need

Our desires guide us. From birth, we seek comfort from outside ourselves. As infants, we seek comfort from our binky. As young children, there are not enough toys to satisfy our wants. This pattern continues into adulthood, varying only in our ability to fulfill them.

Unfortunately, each satisfied want brings only fleeting moments of satisfaction, followed by seemingly long gaps of time filled with ominous daydreaming. We live with a perpetual need for more, as material desires cannot fully satisfy us, and their created expectations are unrealistic.

Our one Indispensable Human Need is that of continual serenity. A serene heart is a grateful heart. Lasting serenity is found when Spirit guides us. Happiness is found in gratitude for what we have.

Suffering results from unfulfilled desires. We waste life energy chasing insignificant wants; instead, we would do well to seek spiritual fulfillment. Once in partnership with Spirit, our Indispensable Human Need will be met. Our material desires will lose significance, suffering will cease, and we will experience everlasting serenity.

April 29

Light of Spirit and Positive Energy

In active addiction, isolation blocks us from the Light of Spirit and Positive Energy. Control, self-will, and self-direction distanced us from others and from a Higher Power.

Our lives became dysfunctional as we tried to control the inevitable crashes and free-falls. Each day, we summoned our will to fight and overcome addiction to chemicals, people, behaviors, or negative thought patterns. But we found that self-reliance was no match for a virus of the mind.

To resolve our difficulties and avoid a life of unbearable misery, we had to seek a power greater than ourselves. A Higher Power gave us rebirth. To heal, we stopped all dysfunctional activity and found our way home to our Inner Survival Instinct.

Once we completely let go of control and self-directed will and welcomed the guidance of others and our inner spiritual resource, we again experienced the Light of Spirit and Positive Energy.

April 30

Father Son and Guiding Spirit

There is a Father, a Son, and a Guiding Spirit within us. The Son symbolizes the child that resides within us throughout our lives. Often, society stifles our childlike innocence in favor of a scripted performance. The child is what's left of our purity; laughter, playfulness, spontaneity and mischief are all products of our inner child.

The child lacks boundaries, so the father provides boundaries or balance to the child's vivacity. The Father provides the Son with the nourishment he needs in the form of praise, love, and teaching.

The Guiding Spirit serves as the channel through which the Father receives direction from the source of Divine Inspiration. The joyful play of the Son and the nurturing of the Father find harmony when they are guided by Spirit.

When the Father, Son, and Guiding Spirit dance as one, we experience the Trilogy on our human journey.

May 1

Spiritual Recovery

A spiritual malady is a dysfunctional relationship with self, others, and the world. This dis-ease manifests itself in destructive behaviors and thought patterns of the mind. At its root is a set of circumstances and interactions aligned to bring about this human calamity.

The act of compulsively using mind-altering substances or behaviors is only one symptom of the malady. There are many other symptoms such as greed, self-loathing, resentment, fear, insecurity, guilt, skepticism, anger, or pessimistic thoughts about ourselves, others, and our lives. What we seek to recover from is a dysfunctional mind made so by social complexities and a lack of connection to the Inner Spirit.

Since we can't change society, we engage in Spiritual Recovery. Healing necessitates an unbroken link with our inner selves, directed by a force greater than our mind—a Divine Higher Power.

No one escapes this life without experiencing the depths of innate suffering. Yet, in seeking the realm of spirit, we will embark on a journey of self-love, compassion, faith, security, shamelessness, trust, good humor, and positive thinking. We will establish and enjoy a daily loving relationship with our inner self and others. We come to experience a deep gratitude for the life we have been given.

May 2

Forgiveness Soothes the Sorrow

Although we don't forget hurtful moments, Forgiveness Soothes the Sorrow. Forgiving is not forgetting. Forgiving is finding a resolution to unchangeable situations.

Too often, we look at situations superficially or one-sidedly. Understanding our role in creating this painful situation could be useful. An honest examination brings to light our contribution to the transgression.

In the heat of the moment, we are in the eye of the storm, blinded by resentment. We must find calm before we enter self-examination. We gain awareness of our wrongs by connecting with our Higher Self, the spirit-consciousness, at the center of our being. We take full responsibility for our actions and forgive ourselves, vowing a sincere desire to refrain from such behavior.

If we conclude we were an innocent participant, then we ask, What purpose does it serve for me to hold on to this bitterness? Does it help me justify my loneliness, my anger, or some other negative behavior? Resentment serves no good purpose. It only serves to tear down our Divine Spirit.

Having forgiven ourselves, we are now ready to forgive the other. When we're committed to forgiveness, our resentment loses all power over us, and future resentments become minor irritations.

Forgiveness leads us to empathic understanding and compassion, which diminishes our hurt and lifts our spirits.

May 3

Regrettable Moments

I have regrets I can't let go of.

The regrets I feel today relate to missed opportunities or wrongdoings of the past. I can learn from their lessons and make amends for my mistakes whenever possible. Anything else is fruitless. Consciously carrying the guilt forward will only serve to justify current misdeeds. Sadly, I've learned mostly from heartache.

When regret presents itself in a thought, I acknowledge its presence and ask for inner forgiveness. Over time, through many humbling moments of acceptance of the regrettable wrong, it does not become forgotten, but the guilt slowly fades.

Today, I am mindful of my actions and allow for spiritual guidance so to take advantage of opportunities that in the past went unrecognized or neglected. In this way, my future will be free of Regrettable Moments.

May 4

The Good Opinion of Others

Abraham Maslow counseled that in order to achieve self-actualization, one must live *"independent of the good opinion of others."*

At first, I conformed to culture's norms. Later, I rebelled against all rules. Finally, I found a balance. My spirit is asking me to trust the beating of my drum. It took the pain and suffering of earlier life stages to shape me into what I have become.

Some judge me by the mistakes and wrongs of my past. I cannot and will not allow the wrong actions of those dark days to define the man I am today. I have found it difficult to completely cut the chains and run free from the enslavement of my past, but with each passing day, I feel the last link nearing exhaustion. Freedom is on the horizon.

By letting go of other people's opinions of me, whether negative or positive, I proclaim my freedom of individuality. Every day, I challenge myself to grow and overcome my imperfections, and though perfection will always elude me, I declare my independence from the Good Opinion of others.

May 5

A Life Beyond My Wildest Dreams

When I first entered recovery, I heard a friend say that sobriety had given him a life beyond his wildest dreams. I questioned his statement because I associated such a life with being a big shot and having material wealth. I could not see such gains in what would become a life of abstinence, doomed to adhere to sober principles.

The starting point presents such challenges, and most people do not stay long enough to experience the gifts of sobriety. They quit five minutes before the miracle. I feel blessed to have stayed long enough to experience freedom from my delusional, grandiose way of thinking.

A life beyond our wildest dreams need not involve material accumulation or personal prestige, which, at best, would provide only superficial well-being. Recovery tasks us with a higher purpose that, through our example, others may know peace.

I am free from compulsion, grateful for my place and purpose, and have an intimate relationship with a loving God of my understanding. I am living A Life Beyond My Wildest Dreams!

May 6

Gaining Personal Integrity

I cannot expect others to change just because I found a desperate need to change.

I gained awareness and insight into my destructive patterns and made honest amends in word and deed, yet I saw limited change in how they judged me. By putting my spiritual knowledge into practice, I regained my personal integrity. I made peace with my wrongs and came to accept the losses. In an unrealistic attempt to gain the approval and forgiveness of others, I would remain hostage to the blame and guilt of my past.

I feel absolved of my sins. I carry only the responsibility of forgiveness and understanding. I have the reasonable expectation of being recognized for who I've become rather than being judged for who I was.

Living with integrity means practicing trustworthiness, selflessness, love, gratitude, and humility. I must accept and forgive the imperfections of others as I have forgiven my own, and trust that in their hearts they recognize my profound transformation.

May 7

Natural Order

Our planet has all the natural resources its inhabitants need to survive. The natural order has an organized sequence, as smooth as a ballroom dance to the beat of a classical philharmonic.

What is not orderly is the human mind. Its only knowledge is of the material world. As man has learned to manipulate natural resources, he has disturbed their purity. The coordinated sequence has slowly put all the instruments out of tune. The rhythm of the dancers has lost its perfect unity.

We communicate with each other through the mind. We debate and formulate new ways of manipulating nature, all in the name of progress. We disagree and quarrel because of our attachment to worldly goods. Man has lost all sense of compromise.

The one thing that has not changed is the human spirit, which remains pure and accessible to all who seek its loving guidance. The solution to all of our world's problems could be solved if we would unite in a spiritual bond, each contributing our small part to the overwhelming task of restoring order to our minds and our world.

May 8

Spiritual Malady

I believe psychosocial addictions are ill-fated methods of coping with, or attempting to, resolve inner unrest.

I was at conflict with my place in the world; I was suffering from a malady of the spirit. Mind-altering substances and behaviors became my solution; they softened my distorted view of reality.

Being restored to sanity assumes physical cessation, psychological rewiring and spiritual practice. I would not have found inner peace without developing a connection to a Higher Power.

Abstinence would have removed some of the chaos from my life, but it would not have healed the conflict within. Only by eradicating mental turmoil will we extinguish the pilot light of the malady.

Refraining from negative behaviors and adhering to spiritual practice sustains long-term recovery. In this way, we experience inner peace and healing from The Spiritual Malady.

May 9

Perfect Equanimity

We claim our needs are unmet. Yet when we inventory our allotments, we find that we have enough love, material possessions, challenges, and solutions to get us through another day.

We often lack a Divine Connection to ourselves, others, and the world. Divine Connection is within our reach. Willingness is the key that opens the door to the spiritual realm. Once open, even just a crack, we can feel the warmth of its light wash over us as tranquility. Through spiritual connection, we increase our gratitude for what we have and become more charitable toward others.

We will undoubtedly benefit from developing or deepening our connection to the Divine Consciousness of the Universe and allowing it to become more present in our daily lives. Through its guidance, we will find Perfect Equanimity between our desires and spiritual needs.

May 10

Hurt Needs a Voice

In moments of calm, we plant the spiritual seeds for harvesting in times of suffering.

Our happiness has a voice. We do not hesitate to share our joy with others. Our hurt also needs a voice. We tend to hold it in as if our suffering is shameful. The longer we hold onto our pain, the more powerful it becomes, and unless we eliminate it, it will spread like wildfire, from our thoughts to our emotions to our physical bodies.

We do not need to hide our hurt. We do not need to keep our suffering a secret. In times of torment, give your hurt a voice. We must share our despair, grief, heartbreak, or remorse to quickly cut its power. Avoid the hesitation of reaching out to others and instead offer them purpose. Gather your harvest of spiritual healing, smother the flames of torment, and place your suffering directly into the loving hands of your God.

Our Higher Power is always present when we call upon Him. The Master and Giver of all Life understands our pain and loves us despite our faults; He knows us well, for we are of His making.

May 11

Allowing for Imperfection

During my darkest days, I was conditioned to believe that I was always "wrong."

I am not who I used to be. I've experienced a spiritual transformation that has made me aware of my negative character traits and motivated me to monitor my daily actions and reactions. I hold myself accountable for misdeeds, yet people and situations trigger old insecurities.

There are people in my life who lack correctness. I've learned to allow them their imperfection. Although I am guided to focus only on my actions, it is acceptable to acknowledge that others can be "wrong."

There are people in our lives who live in spiritual darkness; we can pray for them to awaken, but we cannot absolve them of imperfection or become martyrs for their ills. By shouldering unwarranted blame or guilt, we absolve others of their "wrongness" and dim our spiritual light.

I will not allow the "wrongs" of others to hinder my spiritual progress.

May 12

Living in Harmony

In order to live in harmony, I need to accept different perspectives on all situations; each individual sees life from a different point of view.

Life experiences condition us to unwanted reactions. We are often unaware of circumstances that cause us or others to react in a certain way at a particular time. But this is probably related to past trials or principles we have developed over our lifetime.

There is no wrong viewpoint. When exposed to varying opinions, it is key to remain unbiased and receptive. When guided by goodwill, we find merit in the words and opinions of others.

Accepting that we cannot pretend to know the path another has traveled, encourages us to develop unconditional acceptance, paving the way for harmonious and benevolent interactions

While we want our opinions to be heard, we must also honor differing perspectives.

May 13

Spiritual Calm

Patience takes effort.

Tolerance takes effort.

Spiritual Calm is the reward for our efforts.

Impatience breathes demand; our current chaotic world has become selfish and self-centered. Polite courtesy has been displaced.

Patience breathes appeal; when we can detach from our ego, we request with tender love.

Intolerance breathes anger; our fuses are shortened and we are quick to resent.

Tolerance breathes forgiveness; with empathic understanding we find acceptance of human imperfection.

The material world is pushing us toward increasing conflict. It is slowly tearing at the spiritual fabric that unites us. We have become bitter and confused.

Cultivating compassion through patience and self-tolerance results in increased inner Spiritual Calm.

May 14

A Life of Contentment

Contentment lives in the spaces between life's highs and lows. Contentment is all I seek. I no longer seek excitement and adventure, nor do I allow myself to fall victim to misfortune. My contentment rarely wavers, thanks to my prioritization of acceptance and gratitude as my first emotional responses.

In the past, when I experienced unpleasant emotions, I would default to the role of victim; "Why me?" Though old reactions still surface regularly, I am now aware of negative states of mind and consciously channel acceptance for that which I cannot change and courage to change that which I can.

Euphoric moments are rare, for I am no longer attracted to the thrill of short-term ecstasy. I find comfort in the stillness of the moment and favor long-term serenity.

I have found acceptance and gratitude to be on the path to A Life of Contentment.

May 15

Communion With Spirit

To experience spiritual communion, we must become an open channel to the Spiritual Source. We enter this communion by creating regularity in the time we set aside for prayer and meditation.

With continued practice, we come to realize spiritual presence, calm, guidance, and the assurance that The Unseen Source of All Love cares for us. Our mind becomes attuned to Spirit Consciousness.

This isn't limited to a few. It is available to all of us. Our souls house the guiding light that imbues our lives with meaning and direction.

Love, peace, and tranquility are not permanent in the material realm, but are eternal in our Communion With Spirit.

May 16

The Last Ship Out

I embarked on my Spiritual Journey because it was the last ship to leave the land of hell. Fearful and unsure of where I was going, a small glimmer of hope remained that I wouldn't have to go back.

Arriving at an unfamiliar destination, I found life unrealistically uncomplicated. Basic principles of acceptance, tolerance, and faith replaced the heaviness of my previous beliefs. Awkwardly and very slowly, I adapted to this new way of being.

At first I was clumsy in my words and actions, but with the help of others who had been indoctrinated, I adapted to this new way of life. While it began as mere survival, this way of life became comfortable and preferable.

My desperation was undoubtedly and unconsciously spiritually guided. The leap of faith I took on The Last Ship Out saved me from a life of torturous suffering and introduced me to this new land of the spiritually free.

May 17

The Soft Whisper From Within

A few years ago, I participated in a running challenge—my first in several years. The years add up and my body wasn't as forgiving. I prepared as best I could. At the starting line, my mind launched itself with grandiose delusional thoughts and overconfidence.

The gun blasted, and the race began. I felt great for the first mile. My mind assured me that this would be an easy feat. The soft whisper from within suggested prudence. Running along the narrow, rolling dirt trails, it quickly became clear that this would prove to be more challenging than expected. The second half of the race would test my mental and physical abilities like never before. For the first time in all my years of racing, I had to slow down to walk up some of the unforgiving hills. I was humbled!

At that moment, my delusional thinking changed from "The Great I Am" to "The Great I'm Not," turning into my tormentor. It harshly reminded me of my age, lack of commitment to training, and the absurd decision to take on this challenge. Once again, the soft whisper from within interrupted, this time comforting me with encouragement and praise for my efforts.

In this situation, as in many others, it is the soft whisper from within that can be relied upon to provide discretion and compassion, and to dispel torment and grandiosity from my delusional mind.

May 18

Risking Faith

We do not risk faith because we're afraid that our prayers will go unanswered. Deep down, we fear the silence might mean there's no one listening. That perhaps none of it is real. That maybe God doesn't exist at all.

We only have to look back at our day, week, month, or life to be reminded of the many God-coincidences we have experienced. Life is not defined by big events, but by an accumulation of precious moments. Faith is asking for His Will for us and humbly trusting the outcome. Even if it goes against our mental reasoning.

The timing and manner of answered prayers are determined by God's infinite wisdom, not our expectations. The evidence of His work often goes unnoticed.

May 19

Deception

The expectations of loved ones, society, and cultural norms infiltrate the fragile vulnerability of our youth, shaping our sense of self and how we view the world. Deception takes root fertile ground of self-doubt and shame.

My deception started when I panicked about not meeting perceived expectations. I failed compared to others' intelligence, wealth, ethnicity, or life experiences. Our minds create the most powerful shame.

Shame led to protection through deception. As my dishonesty grew, my shame obscured what light was left of my self-worth. The path of deception is mined with explosive self-destruction.

Recovering my integrity took less effort than the all-consuming years of deception. Through my daily spiritual practice, my cloud of shame slowly faded. Only the scars remain as a daily reminder.

Today, I recognize when shame is approaching and instead of using deception, I proudly carry my Truth and accept that I am all that my Creator intended me to be.

May 20

Detachment From Hurt

I allow people access to my emotional vulnerabilities, which leads to excessive hurt. Because my heart is vulnerable, I experience sorrow. I do not need to close the door on my vulnerability, only on my expectations.

My deepest wounds come from those I love most, stemming from my unfounded belief in their flawlessness and the false notion that love causes no hurt.

My hurt results from my lack of perspective and empathy. My vulnerability clouds my recognition of the humanity of others. When I feel hurt or betrayed, I examine my unrealistic expectations. There, I find the root cause of the chain reaction leading to my disillusionment.

In matters of the heart, expectations are the villains that breed despondency. Allowing others to be flawed, disables the triggers. Resulting in detachment from hurt and for uninterrupted love and understanding.

May 21

Lasting Happiness

My happiness depended on the perception of how others viewed and judged my performance. In this way, I experienced only fleeting moments of pure joy because external conditions were rarely ideal.

Pure, unadulterated happiness begins within. Entering into a relationship with our Higher Power plants the seeds of inner peace, which in turn allows our relationships with others to flourish.

The quality of our relationship with our Higher Power determines our happiness. Our spiritually guided actions inspire us to live worthy, purposeful lives and surrender all self-judgment to a Higher Source.

Harvesting our inner peace brings about Lasting Happiness.

May 22

Situations with Solutions

Each day upon awakening, I devote some quiet time to acknowledging the presence of my Divine Father and to express gratitude for inner spiritual guidance. I preview the day ahead and then set out to fulfill my earthly obligations.

Inevitably, I am confronted with the daily turbulence of the material realm. My earlier experience of divine calm slowly fades because of these. With my delusional mind in motion, I respond to unpleasant experiences or thoughts with seemingly uncontrollable responses.

In these moments, I pause to reflect upon the morning's acknowledgements and request of my Spiritual Guide that I be steered away from unflattering reactions.

Inner spiritual guidance directs me to view worldly problems as Situations with Spiritual Solutions. We can overcome all obstacles in the spiritual realm.

Comfort can be found in knowing that the Inner Spirit will guide us through any of life's unavoidable challenges.

(Dedicated to Jimmy S.)

May 23

My Healing

My earthly conditioning prioritized material wealth and social status above all else. In recovery, I awoke to a new reality and understood what is most meaningful.

I now see clearly that the illusory pursuit of material success is destroying our perception of the world, ourselves, and contributing to our dishonor of one another.

The root cause of my malady wasn't the chemical addictions or compulsive behaviors themselves, but a deep, negative response to the physical world—one that led me away from authenticity and disconnected me from my true self.

For my healing to truly begin, I first needed to recover from my addictive patterns and embrace a spiritual program of recovery. Only then did I gain the clarity to understand what I had become, who I wanted to be, and where I hoped to go.

May 24

Reconciliation

My material mind and spiritual soul are polar opposites living together within my being. Dis-ease caused them to drift apart, a consequence of ignoring spiritual guidance during years of immoral and reckless behavior. As in any other broken relationship, reconciliation necessitates the rebuilding of trust.

The soul understands and forgives a misguided past. While spirituality and materialism have found some common ground, my mind relentlessly revisits the past, punishing me with memories of what I fled.

I am not a conformist, but a rebel against societal norms that dismantle individuality in favor of outdated cultural values with an exaggerated emphasis on material success.

As my trust of spiritual guidance deepened, my mind's tight grip on the material realm softened. It was only through spiritually guided recovery that my material mind and spiritual soul finally reconciled.

May 25

Time Takes time

I plant a seedling and, in my impatience, expect it to bear fruit the very next day. Nurturing takes patience, growing takes time, blooming is just the end result.

I have often given up on ideas, and life projects because I was driven to demand instant gratification. I had to learn to give Time, time.

As a teenager, I took music lessons in guitar, keyboard, and bass. I quit after only a few sessions because I didn't see any immediate progress. Only through my spiritually guided recovery could my material mind and spiritual soul be reconciled. I wished to speed up Time!

I went to college with the intention of eventually going to law school. Seven years seemed too dear a commitment, so I dropped out. I was young and impetuous and unwilling to give Time, time!

I am grateful that I exercised restraint in early recovery because the climb back to sanity seemed long and arduous. The elders wished me a long, slow recovery, assured me of success, and informed me that Time would take time!

By allowing Time, time to heal, time to connect with myself, time to learn who I am, the spiritual seedling within me grew in strength and resilience. Even though it's been years, decades, I have not yet arrived. The focus of my recovery is on my journey, not my destination. I am patient now because I have accepted that Time Takes time!

May 26

Polarities of the Soul

I am often conflicted by the Polarities of my Soul; my heart and mind are often at odds. It's a battle between the free spirit and the bondage of conditioning.

Sadly, most of the time, I played it safe and allowed my conditioned mind to win over my less wise and immature heart. Parental and societal influences trumped spontaneity. I felt trapped.

I took the first train out of that reality. Escapism freed me from a rigid, dictatorial, mundane, programmed lifestyle. These were reckless times with disastrous results.

Finding balance felt unattainable. I seemed to be in a constant emotional tug-of-war. Somewhere deep within, I held the power to end the struggle and follow the quiet, persistent voice of my heart. However, I found myself unable to risk the betrayal of the status quo.

My shortsightedness withheld my courage to take risks for what I desired and step into the unknown. Awareness is only the first phase in a predictable rebellion.

May 27

The Journey of Recovery

The Shadow

What I dislike most in others is connected to experiences that I have lived, repressed, and now make up my dark side. They are my shadow.

Just as important as manifesting my light is gaining awareness and acknowledging that there is darkness within me. Character traits that I am ashamed of, but thoughtlessly project onto others.

My anger, resentment, or jealousy toward another is based on actions in my past that resulted in shame. Past experiences intensify present emotional states.

Awareness of my shadow calms impulsive reactions. Ignoring jagged personality traits allows them to flourish. By embracing my darkness, I create change. By ignoring my darkness, I allow it to continue to exist.

I become tolerant of what I strongly dislike in others by recognizing and accepting it as my own.

As much as I would like to ignore my dark side, it is only by acknowledging it that I will lessen my judgment of others.

(This was my interpretation of the Jungian Shadow)

May 28

The Little Pencil

"I am a little pencil in the hand of a writing God who is sending a love letter to the world." Mother Theresa

It is in the golden silence of the early morning, and only after I have set my spiritual intention, that I reach for my pen and pad. I seek to allow the Spiritual Source to guide my words.

Throughout the day, I try to stay connected to the inner spirit to dispel mental disturbances. Divine Consciousness is present in all aspects of our lives; in every interaction, thought, and action. It is only through spiritual practice that we come to experience its favor.

I have established self-imposed expectations for living a Spirit-driven life. In my commitment, I find increasing stability in my mental and spiritual states. Although I am not asked for perfection, I am held accountable for my efforts.

Each of us is a little pencil, and as such, we want to contribute to this love letter to the world by practicing kindness and humility toward one another. This is best accomplished when guided by a Spiritual Source.

May 29

Distractions

There are endless distractions that I allow to interrupt the natural flow of my day. It seems that I don't allow enough time to complete a task. There is always another distraction to break my focus.

Social media, the Internet, and television are fierce enemies of spiritual calm. They present alternatives to a mind that seeks escape. My mind tries to unburden me from the present moment by finding a distraction, only to punish me later for my negligence.

Only the Spirit has the power to calm the mind. When the Spirit is unsettled, the mind finds a distraction. Eliminating or reducing the time spent on social media, which leads to judgment by comparison, or being hypnotized by one of the endless mind twisters on the illusion screen, could be invested in nurturing my Spirit.

Time escapes my grasp, it runs at a rapid pace. I will do well to consider the amount lost to unworthy distractions and seek balance to allow the Spirit time to calm my unruly mind.

May 30

Anger

Anger is as addictive and destructive as any chemical or behavioral compulsion, for it too offers an escape from undesirable states of mind.

When compulsions are removed, emotions rise to fill the void. Anger fed compulsion, compulsion fed anger. A vicious, destructive cycle that prevents the guidance of a loving Spirit. Anger does not allow for the concept of forgiveness. Addiction desperately tries to block all alternatives to recovery.

In a moment of clarity, desire takes a breath and the process of change begins. Desire needs a way; a program, a practice, a path to travel to slowly shed its heaviness. All roads lead to self-awareness and spiritual understanding.

We become lighter as we let go of what has been weighing us down. We become free of our anger and other compulsions by surrendering to a new way of living, in which insight develops and relief is abundant.

May 31

Stoke the Fire of Love

We are all cut from the same cloth. If we surrender to Spiritual Order, we will live in harmony.

Outwardly, we have different views and ideas. But inwardly, we all yearn for love and security.

Outwardly, we project actions and reactions created by a mind that is easily influenced by matters of the ego. Inwardly, we are guided by Creation, by Divine Consciousness, by that which is not seen but which unites and completes us.

We should seek guidance from the Spiritual Source to dispel outward negativity and instill humility that will Stoke the Fire of Love in our hearts.

June 1

Lost in Darkness

When it became apparent life would not cooperate with my fantasy-making mind, I sought shelter from its exuberant demands. The cave did not have all the comforts of home, but it provided a safe zone for my arrogant ignorance.

I acknowledged the danger, but I could still see the light and could choose to turn back at any time. As the seasons changed, the chill in my heart grew colder and I was driven deeper into the cavernous mountain of darkness.

I lost track of time and direction. By the time I decided to turn around, it was too late. I'd lost my mind in the maze of dark tunnels of insanity. I had surrendered my power of choice and became conditioned to accept darkness as my fate.

Tomorrow, I will reach out for light!

June 2

Guided to the Light

Lost in a deranged state of mind, I wandered blindly in the deep tunnels of insanity. I lost all hope and became conditioned to this way of existence.

Divine intervention interceded, and my broken spirit suddenly spied a ray of light up above. I summoned the courage and strength to climb a jagged rock face toward the bright blue sky.

My spirit found freedom when a moment of clarity overcame evil.

My rebirth demands constant vigilance against temptation and disregard for my spiritual goal, for I receive only a daily reprieve.

To keep this new way of life going, I have a duty to share my story and inspire others to find their way to the light.

June 3

Principles Before Personalities

Principles make up the moral fiber of the goodness and kindness we're intended to show one another. Our upbringing instills fundamental rules about what is and isn't acceptable behavior.

In allowing for spiritual guidance, we live a principled life.

Personalities are made up of learned behaviors and emotional and social survival skills related to life experiences. Nurtured beings learn love and un-nurtured beings learn hurt.

Being receptive to Spiritual guidance helps overcome hurt and restore inner peace.

Our personalities are ruled by a king or queen ego. We define ourselves as being a certain way and become conditioned, even attached, to our identified way of being. Our character is self-directed and tainted by excessive desires for accumulation or status that disrupt, overshadow, and deceive our charitable hearts.

Love and compassion are at the core of human nature. As we move from self-direction to spiritual guidance, our first inclination toward another becomes empathic understanding; this is how we come to place Principles Before Personalities.

June 4

Paralysis by Analysis

My life was in shambles. The light of my spirit was dim. I lived in the shadows of existence.

Through what I can only describe as a moment of Divine Intervention, a ray of light shone upon me and a warm glimmer of hope melted my resistance. I had a spiritual experience, although I knew of no such thing at the time.

This awakening to Divine Consciousness provided an inner solution that freed me from my nightmare. All my previous efforts, intellectual power, well-intentioned plans, and empty promises had always fallen short.

I recognized this experience as a miracle of the spirit. Inquiry brought no substantial answers; things of the spirit preclude logic. I did not know what I had found or its spiritual value, but I knew I was not going back.

Many people become paralyzed by overanalyzing the simplicity of recovery. Though they have no solution themselves, they are overwhelmed by doubt, resistance, and disbelief when they hear of spiritual conversion.

Paralysis by Analysis is a lack of faith in what the mind cannot conceive. Miracles have no logical explanation. Clarity comes through unexplainable channels. We would do well to cherish this rarest of blessings.

June 5

The Process

Few of us began this journey as believers. Sheer desperation forged our initial bond. We had exhausted all alternatives. Embarking on this ambiguous path was neither logical nor predictable, but it was the last train out.

At first, my Higher Power was The Process itself. My strength came from witnessing the radiance of my fellow travelers. In time, the landscape revealed a spiritual purity that I had not fathomed. It was while walking the path and living The Process that I met my Spiritual Guide and became a believer.

The Process embraces everyone who is troubled. This process heals disturbances, simultaneously training sufferers to become potential healers. The light of the Healing Spirit is within all of us and shines brightest when shared selflessly with others.

It is through embarking on The Process that each believer will find that in which to place his or her trust and faith. Through The Process, we learn that suffering is optional, and we heal by communing with one another.

June 6

A Spiritual Experience

A Spiritual Experience comes about through an act of Prayer.

An act of Prayer is a request for guidance from The Omnipotent Spirit of the Universe, for Realistic Visualization, and for the Manifestation of Pure Intention.

A Realistic Visualization is our true and desired result.

Manifestation is the process by which we will contribute to the outcome.

Pure intention is that which is for the benefit of others.

A Spiritual Experience is our answered Prayer.

June 7

Eliminating Aftershocks

The experiences of our youth deeply conditioned our minds. Some have blindly relied on maladaptive coping skills to survive their troubled developmental years.

It is impossible to change the past. However, past experiences impact our minds when triggered by similar present circumstances. These influences are often subconscious, making us unaware that we may be involuntarily reacting to an incident that is influenced by an event from our past.

We often punish ourselves unnecessarily for unacceptable, unintended reactions to others. These may result from past events that have festered into resentment, guilt, or shame. We have little choice; they are pre-conditioned responses.

By developing spiritually guided insight into our past, it begins to lose power over our present. Only then can we recondition our minds so that yesterday's tremors do not return as today's aftershocks.

By acknowledging how we came to be, we can change who we are and who we will become.

June 8

The 12 Stepper

Recovery is a large, multilayered, delicious cake. We want to dive unapologetically into the middle and get our fill. We achieve this by putting to use the advice of those who came before us and found inner peace.

Lacking in meeting attendance, sponsorship, step work, service to the group, or prayer and meditation, distances us from the fellowship, the program, and from a relationship with our Higher Power.

We're walking in the periphery of recovery. Settling for crumbs. Loitering with intent to recover. We may stay abstinent, but we're missing out on the fullness of Sobriety which consists of making a total reversal from who we were as selfish addicts or alcoholics to selfless humble servants.

If you're doing what is suggested, keep on. If you're lacking, take action to get yourself back on the road to becoming Happy, Joyous, and Free.

For a healthy sobriety, be a 12 Stepper!

Don't be a crumb snatcher!

June 9

Outing Spiritual Beliefs

Outing my spiritual beliefs brings with it a sense of responsibility. I must walk the walk, otherwise my words lose meaning and may even discourage those who receive them with hope. Most importantly, I must remain accountable to my ideals while accepting my inability to live a flawless life.

The hurtful experiences that are engraved in my mind often overwhelm the patience, kindness, or peace that is present in my heart. In my weakest moments I bring shame to my ideal. The process from having faith to living faith requires selflessness for it to grow. But only time will bring it to maturity.

The ongoing development of my spiritual self serves to heal, learn, and grow from inherent human suffering. Spiritual healing has involved taking a risk and exposing my beliefs, but this risk is another incentive to hold myself accountable to the ideals set forth by my Higher Power.

June 10

Seeking Shelter

Twelve-step meetings have grown in number and popularity worldwide since their inception in 1935. The first of these meetings had only two participants. They found fellowship through identification, faith through prayer, and purpose through service. This model has endured and continues to thrive in its ability to provide shelter from mental, physical, and spiritual maladies.

A Twelve-Step meeting offers protection from unpleasant emotions, disturbing circumstances, feelings, or thoughts that disturb our peace through spiritual treatment. The program provides instructions for living by developing a relationship with a power greater than our mind.

Finding shelter from the storm does not need to be an organized event. Once equipped with spiritual knowledge, we open our spiritual umbrella at our convenience; anytime, anywhere, by finding refuge through harmony with a Higher Power of our choosing. Overcoming life's most challenging hurdles is easier when surrounded by support, faith, and selfless acts while being in tune with the Divine Spirit of the Universe.

June 11

Honor Humanness

There is merit in all human beings. After all, we are all children of the Great Spirit.

For someone to experience my love, I must fully accept them as they are and have no illusions that they need to change. That choice lies only at their feet.

I intend to refrain from any form of judgment or criticism. Should these arise, empathy will replace them. I intend to see life from the perspective of my friends' human experiences to understand better how they came to be.

I do not have to agree with or even like all people. I must, however, value their humanity and cherish their individuality. There is spirit in all of us. I look to that spirit in all beings and become fully present to honor their unique worth.

June 12

Compromise and Understanding

We want to feel that we are at the center of the hearts of those closest to us. There are times in which we can feel them withdrawing. Although it may be unintentional, or perhaps even for our protection, we feel rejected. When in this emotional state, it is best to pause because immediate reactive reactions cause shame and further hurt.

The timing of expressing our feelings is crucial. We must be calm and find our friend or partner free to listen. Our expressions of love are careful and sincere; we use "I" statements to avoid assigning blame.

The outcome is unpredictable. They might not be immediately receptive, perhaps even defensive. If so, we understandably withdraw and honor them with space and time for resolution. Where there is love, there is also Compromise and Understanding. Time is a great equalizer. We will have done our part to be transparent about our feelings so that resentment does not fester.

Honesty in our relationships means taking risks by being open with one another. We follow love's guidance, trusting that honesty will bring similar honesty. We take responsibility for our efforts and surrender the outcome to The Spiritual Source.

June 13

Humanity – Spirituality

Humanity is a predictable means to an end!

Our intention is to secure comfort and happiness. Our plans, influenced by society's implied achievements, define our human successes and failures.

Living plugged into humanity is exhausting. It drains us mentally and emotionally. Escaping our daily routines is possible by connecting with our inner selves.

Humanity is doing!

Spirituality is experiencing presence! Spirit's purpose is to help us understand our humanity. It helps us find a balance between the exuberance of success and the heartbreak of failure. It prevents us from giving undue importance to either of these polar opposites. In those fleeting moments when we are fully in the moment, sacredly connected to our inner spirit, we encounter such neutrality.

Spirituality is Being!

Humanity serves our sentient needs.

Spirituality serves our metaphysical needs.

In balance, we discover Comfort and Happiness.

June 14

The Pink Cloud

The process of recovery rewarded me with infinite light.

When I first tasted the sweet nectar of sobriety, I could not have imagined the gifts it would bring. Every morning, upon awakening, I am grateful for the freedom from excruciating physical, moral, or emotional pain.

After many years of self-imposed isolation from people, places, and things, this new dimension of life is like the first breath upon returning to the surface from a deep dive into ocean waters.

From the very first day, I floated effortlessly on a Pink Cloud; the feeling that accompanies the first conscious contact with Divine Energy, a liberating sensation, free of suffering. There were warnings that this, too, would pass.

Although the Pink Cloud may be temporarily obscured in moments of surrender to self-will, delusion, or weakness, it is unconditionally within my grasp. It is maintained by consistent gratitude, humility, and praise for the opportunity of a new beginning.

I do not allow negativity to linger. I dress up and show up daily, with commitment and confidence that the Divine Power within will guide me on a purposeful journey.

In this way, the Pink Cloud will be everlasting.

June 15

Do No Harm

When experiencing anger or hurt, first, Do No Harm.

Negative actions or malicious thoughts toward another to quell our burning resentments may provide temporary satisfaction but will eventually boomerang as shame or guilt. They will not remedy our intention and will increase our discomfort. Negative actions and thoughts block the path to serenity. The harm we inflict on another as justified retaliation steals our peace.

We experience anger and hurt—unavoidable human emotions—with reasonable minds and serenity of spirit, but only if we rise above our defensive impulses. We overcome resentment through understanding, compassion, and forgiveness for others and ourselves.

When moments of anger or hurt persist, rather than retaliating we pause to ensure that we will first Do No Harm.

June 16

A New Way of Being

We've Adapted to a New Way of Being.

Some may appreciate our changes, but there will be misunderstandings of our new rituals. Prayer, meditation, assertiveness, and gratitude may all be cliché and foreign to most "civilians." Living this way goes against the norm of a fast-paced, stressed filled society.

Any questioning of our new way must not sway us, for we may again experience estrangement. We will come to know a new self and be amazed by the modest words we speak, the encouraging thoughts we think, and the new soothing feelings we feel.

If we again feel like outsiders, it will serve us well to spend time with others walking our same path. Contact with like-minded individuals, helps us to feel a part of this new spiritual mosaic. Life will find balance and in time we will feel comfortable around the naysayers and the nonbelievers.

We do not preach or think ourselves superior. We have not gained moral authority. Each morning we slip on our new loose-fitting character and model love, acceptance, and calm. In this way, without a spoken word, we exemplify our New Way of Being.

June 17

Calming The Storms

Faith is a natural way to calm the storms that pass through our minds. In the middle of a calm day, brightened by a blue sky, gusty winds can blow, the sky can darken, and I can experience paralyzing fear. I inventory the moment and my recent past and cannot identify the source of this sudden change in mood and outlook. I desperately try to let go of the fear and escape.

Long ago, the only escape was through chemical or behavioral mind alteration. I could temporarily numb myself and escape unpleasant realities. In doing so, I attracted additional, unintended, and unwanted chaos. Inevitably, reality caught up with me, as this had been a failed human solution.

Today, I find solace in my faith that the storm will pass, as so many have before. Developing faith is the spiritual solution to the inevitable reality that storms and blue skies are cyclical events in our lives.

June 18

The Process of Healing

Whatever the circumstances or reason for embarking on the process of mental, physical, or spiritual healing, we have recognized a need for change. Our suffering commonly leads us to create change. Once the crisis has passed, we often abandon the process.

Recovery requires discipline, and we cannot allow too many other commitments to get in the way. Temptation is daunting, sneaky, and insidious. Not investing in our wellness brings negative returns.

Committing to healing is the easy part; sticking to it is the ultimate challenge. We need to find internal and external strategies to increase motivation and discipline to replace temptation and procrastination.

It is in maintenance that recompense becomes apparent, for here the effort of our exercise, meditation, diet, abstinence, or prayer is rewarded in the form of a healthier body, a clearer mind, and a liberated spirit.

June 19

Spiritual Contemplation

What if we came to believe that there is a guardian spirit, a protector, watching over each of us? Spiritual curiosity leads to spiritual contemplation, and mere contemplation is the prerequisite for growing faith.

What do we have to lose by opening our hearts to the possibility of this existence? Should He not be, we are left as we are. Should She be, we may be relieved of pressures, expectations, and dreaded delusional projections that cause our mind worry and agitation. The feeling may free us from the grief of loss as we consider that our loved ones are in the embrace of their Keeper.

As we open our hearts to spiritual contemplation, we find continued freedom from the emotions and delusions that exist in the material world but have no place in the realm of the spirit.

June 20

Self-Will Run Riot

After years of living by self-will run riot, misusing my power of choice and decency of being, I cannot expect spiritual order to be restored without a resurrection of moral values.

Once recovery begins, we quickly expect everything to be forgotten: "It was all a terrible mistake," "We're back to pick up the pieces." We must not minimize the damage and hurt we have caused to those around us, our character, and our reputation.

My reintegration from a selfish twenty-year walkabout was best accomplished by taking baby steps and living patiently, one day at a time. Connecting with the Great Reality restored my strength, corrected my character, and renewed my reputation.

To remain free from distractions and wasteful living, I will allow for spiritual guidance so that I may live within the bounds of morality, humility, and selflessness.

June 21

Selflessness

Selflessness also brings regret, but only when it feels used by others; when our credo is to put others first, and we receive nothing in return, we feel cheated.

Expecting something in return is not selflessness. True selflessness is a charitable act for the sole purpose of benefiting others. It seeks no reward.

Spiritual inner calm and a serene mind compensate selflessness.

These define our character.

June 22

Divine Intent

I cannot pretend to know the Divine Intent for the world. However, I am certain that we have lost our way. Spiritual inner calm and a serene mind compensate for selflessness.

I imagine that the original design was for all organisms to share in the planet's magnificent natural resources. Over time, humans have consumed, damaged, or destroyed everything intended for the earth's survival.

The distractions of the material world monopolize our attention and divert us from our spiritual purpose. Each individual can accept spiritual guidance and thus refrain from destruction, greed, or jealousy.

I, you, all of us have the ability to listen to the hushed guiding message of the Unseen Spirit, find our way back, and contribute to the fulfillment of Divine Intent.

June 23

The Adult and The Child

The adult in us, filled with pride and expectation, plays the game of life, keeping track of his wins and losses. There are deadlines and performance quotas to meet. Life is spent in pursuit of illusory fulfillment. The adult allows outcomes to define their self-worth.

The child in us has no quotas or expectations to fulfill. It lives in a world of limitless possibilities. The purpose of a child's game is simply to play. There is no winner, no loser, and no consequence. He lives free from the judgment of his value.

A child lives for the moment. One moment, she is happy; the next moment, she is scared; the next moment, she is sad; and the next, she is happy again. Each day she flows freely, experiencing all her emotions.

We all have an adult and a child within, and both serve a purpose. The key is to find a balance between meeting our adult responsibilities and allowing the playfulness and joy of our inner child to be present. Let him bring his freedom from conformity and infuse our daily routines with levity and playfulness. In this way, we will live a fulfilled life.

June 24

Seeking Approval

Change does not beget change!

It is disappointing that I have gained awareness and insight into my destructive patterns and behaviors. I made amends by word or deed, and yet I haven't received the forgiveness I expected.

I cannot remove the blame or guilt of my past by trying to gain the approval or forgiveness of others. It was naive to think that those around me would change their view, and presumptuous to expect that they should.

Different perspectives shaped how people experienced our interactions, resulting in varied interpretations. I am responsible for not selfishly assuming the thoughts or feelings of others or the degree of hurt my malady cast on them.

It is best that I only ask the Great Thinker to hear my prayers, and, in his infinite wisdom, grant forgiveness as he sees fit, for only he knows Truth.

June 25

Move a Muscle Change a Thought

When I experience extreme gloom and feel the world is closing in on me, my mind travels to dangerous cliffs. Self-pity and hopelessness are no longer acceptable states of mind, so I take action. By moving a muscle, I change a thought.

I've discovered that exercise changes my brain chemistry and, as a result, my mood. It helps me shake off the "poor me" blues. We all have to find the physical activity that works best for us. Running is the most effective for me, but a long walk is also beneficial, as it takes me out of my physical environment and distracts me from my pessimism.

Other alternatives for interrupting our thoughts or feelings include attending a recovery meeting, calling a supportive friend or family member, engaging in prayer or meditation.

Inaction and procrastination may feel safe in the moment, but when we ignore our negative emotional states, they often intensify, leaving us more vulnerable to impulsive or irrational decisions. By moving a muscle we change a thought and thus shift consciousness and shed light on our moment of darkness.

June 26

The Way Out

Hitting bottom is a direct consequence of our dis-ease. It can manifest in several ways: addiction, eating disorders, compulsive behaviors, financial devastation, family discord, unemployment, depression, imprisonment, institutionalization, homelessness, and, tragically, death. The list is long.
In these we often differ.

My bottom brought excruciating emotional pain. Guilt and shame overwhelmed me. Gloom and hopelessness accompanied these. I could not imagine living like this, nor could I imagine living any other way.
In these we share similarities.

In finding identification with one another, we can recover from our terminal uniqueness and the loneliness of our souls. Though our bottoms may appear quite different, in our likeness and our spiritual bonding, we find The Way Out.

June 27

The Whisper Within

The Whisper Within offers guidance for overcoming all obstacles that interfere with our serenity. Unfortunately, we ignore that within us, that we cannot explain. We favor our mind over the unseen spirit.

What if we allowed ourselves to be guided by our inner voice?

Perhaps the burden of carefully calculating every life choice would be gone. We would know peace if we could find the courage to allow guidance from the Inner Spiritual Source.

The Whisper Within is as real as any thought that arises in our mind. However, it is softer in tone and gentler in intent. Its purity and love guide us to inner peace.

June 28

The Hollow Inside

The sanctuary of our soul is the place where the purity of our humanity resides.

When the sanctuary is hollow, we are deprived of completeness and desperately seek to fill the void. We are not particular; food, substances, romance, shopping, gambling, smoking, power, pride, and prestige, all can give us a momentary illusion of wholeness.

The source of Eternal Perfection sits quietly at the door of our soul, awaiting our call. It is available to us through spiritual practice. When the Spiritual Source fills the void within with pure unconditional love, momentary illusions are dispelled and we come to know completeness.

June 29

Letting Go

Trying to control situations as if we were puppeteers will inevitably lead to deep disappointment. We are not in charge!

We must be prepared to let go of people, places, and things, for to hold on to what is free, is a vain attempt to keep it from its intended destiny, if only for a moment.

Letting Go does not mean that we will no longer have them in our lives; it means we care enough to respect their choice. It is moments like these that interrupt our breathing, cause our heartbeat to slow and fear to gain an edge because we are afraid to loose control over someone or something. Control we never really had.

Impermanence is the ultimate outcome for all of us. We should live each day free from the paralyzing task of holding on to our preconceived notions of how, when, what, and where and allow the mysteries of life to unfold effortlessly.

In controlling, we interfere with predestined outcomes.

It is in letting go that we set free that which is meant to be.

June 30

Eternal Spirit

Our spirit is alive for all eternity.

Our nature as transient beings is such that there comes a time for a final farewell. Some years ago, suddenly and without notice, someone I loved very much left this material world for the unknown, but her spirit remains. Her spirit lives within me, for I was born of her body and soul.

In my grief, I shed a tear of regret for what was left unsaid, for what was left undone. Life's hardships brought conflict and when we separated not all was resolved. I find comfort in my childhood memories where our bond was without judgement; our love was pure and unconditional.

In my most challenging times, I knew you were hurting with me. Your love was my comfort, and you found your greatest joy in my brightest moments.

I honor your life and your courage on this day, which marks your birthday. Though you have left on your eternal voyage, your spirit remains alive in all I do. For I came from you.

Reflections on Anniversary Month

July 1

Count Down to a Miracle (9 days)

My Truth

When I was a young boy, in my dreams, everything was possible. Everything was attainable. As I grew and shared about my ambitions, the discouraging feedback I interpreted from people, culture, and society was that they were delusional impossibilities. My options became limited as I conformed to that belief.

I was not aware of the sadness that was growing in my spirit. I became vulnerable and incorrigible. Just then, a sweet temptation to escape my sad, dreamless reality presented itself. It was a cunning, False Prophet, luring me, promising me that all my dreams could, indeed, come true. I followed its cunning melody into the darkness, and soon I was lost. Though I tried, I could not find my way back. Years of spiritual turmoil followed this willful abduction.

My Truth was stifled.

July 2

The Journey of Recovery

Reflections on Anniversary Month

Count Down to a Miracle (8 days)

The Origin of My Dis-ease

The dis-ease began long before the arrival of its mental and physical manifestations. The False Prophet began his work when I was still a child. He entered my being through cracks of self-doubt.

Early on, some considered me a golden child. For a while, I could do no wrong. As I reached adolescence, my efforts went unnoticed. I felt unappreciated by those whose attention I sought most. I was unwisely trusted to self-guidance.

I adapted to being a young boy in a foreign land by disguising my Truth. I began to identify what I found shameful about myself. Fears and insecurities grew in my mind. My real self gradually became overshadowed by an impostor, an actor. A void opened in my soul.

The blind search for reassurance had its origin in this dis-ease.

July 3

Reflections on Anniversary Month

Count Down to a Miracle (7 days)

The Nectar of The Gods

I trudged along, doing the necessary footwork to achieve the lofty but realistic goals I had set for myself. The result I sought was recognition through prestige and material wealth—an obviously self-serving path.

It was then, with many years of work still ahead of me, that I was introduced to the Nectar of the Gods. Mind altering substances were the work of the False Prophet, and they immediately provided everything I was seeking.

They transformed me into The Great I Am. A legend of my mind, with the added benefits of numbing self-doubt, the ability to evade effort and responsibility, and tuned out the pesky voices of logic and reason. Believing my pony to be a thoroughbred, I was off to the races.

The delusional mind, under the spell of greatness, exercises reckless judgment.

The Journey of Recovery

July 4

Reflections on Anniversary Month

Count Down to a Miracle (6 days)

Kneeling Before the Master

I had promised myself over and over again that tomorrow I would do things differently, and yet I found myself once again kneeling before that which had become my master.

Disease is an unanticipated virus of the mind and an obstacle to spiritual connection. It took me by surprise. Family and friends tried to make me aware of it, but I did not heed their warnings. Suddenly, one day, I saw the transformation in the mirror. It stole my dignity, honesty, and grace.

The disease had become my master, and although it seemed beneficial and manageable for a while, it eventually became corrosive and disrupted all aspects of my life. I had lost my way.

A cunning, baffling, and powerful False Prophet had infiltrated the core of my being.

July 5

Reflections on Anniversary Month

Count Down to a Miracle (5 days)

Not a Choice!

Many say addiction is a choice. It is Not a Choice!

Why would anyone want to be seen as a derelict or a parasite on society? If it was a conscious choice, then the one making it must be approaching delirium. This was never a choice of my making, and the fun had long ceased to exist.

I had become an outsider looking in, someone who had apparently chosen a morally corrupt way of life. They could not understand my desperate desire to end the nightmare. There was no escape until the False Prophet had squeezed all sense of dignity out of my character. What I had once considered a blessing had become an unbearable curse. The desire to live another day faded.

The despair became real soon after I lost the power of choice.

July 6

Reflections on Anniversary Month

Count Down to a Miracle (4 days)

Shame and Self-pity

The Frosty Mug became my temple, the False Prophet my guiding light.

I lived as an imposter. A white knight by day, a thin lost duke by night.

From our barstool, my cohorts and I lamented the injustices of being misunderstood by an unjust world in which we felt unwanted. We chased instant gratification, oblivious to our impact on those who cared about us. Such is the nature of the disease. It is a treacherous slow dance with the devil that ends with a soft kiss of spiritual death.

Brief moments of reality were followed by delusional speculation. The dis-ease grew stronger. The cross of Shame and Self-pity grew heavier.

"The darkest hour is just before the dawn."

July 7

Reflections on Anniversary Month

Count Down to a Miracle (3 days)

The Hijacking

The False Prophet, who had so graciously provided a solution to all the injustices of my life by introducing me to various magic potions, suddenly turned against me.

I came to realize that I'd been a willing participant in his hijacking of my mind, allowing him to rob me of my dreams, aspirations, regard for family and friends, and most of all, my self-respect. Still, I couldn't imagine a life other than the one I knew. I had grown deep roots in barren soil, and my life bore no fruit.

Of my own will, I had not the power to overcome this malady of the spirit that had been so methodically instilled in me. It wanted my soul and almost had it but for one last desperate whisper from within: "This is not your life; there is a higher purpose for you. . ."

A miracle was in the making.

July 8

Reflections on Anniversary Month

Count Down to a Miracle (2 days)

The Last Debacle

It was supposed to be a social Thursday afternoon that began with the usual self-promise of moderation but quickly spiraled out of control. There was no rhyme or reason, no identifiable emotion to escape. There was no longer need for a fuse, there was only spontaneous combustion.

The light of reason was quickly extinguished and I was unknowingly off on my last debacle. There are snapshots, but no moving images recorded in my memory. The False Prophet had become accustomed to erasing the surveillance tape to keep me from any sense of awareness. No evidence or recollection of the shameful behavior of another mindless episode.

As the light of my consciousness slowly came back on and reality set in, the familiar self-pity of the morning after had inexplicably, miraculously given way to an unfamiliar serenity and hope. The False Prophet had become over-confident, and in his carelessness he had underestimated the power of Good.

A miracle is that which has no logical explanation.

July 9

Reflections on Anniversary Month

Count Down to a Miracle (1 day)

Two Angels

I thought everyone had given up on me, such is the devious nature of the malady. It wanted to condemn my spirit to a life of solitary confinement. We become easy prey when we are isolated.

When the spirit cried out for help on my behalf, help came in the form of two angels who eagerly joined forces and gave freely of themselves so that I might experience grace.

Regardless of my muddied exterior, deep within, the blurred pilot light of the spirit flickered resiliently as a beacon visible to these two angels who prominently featured in my life-changing event. They remembered the good that I had long forgotten.

Through them, my Higher Power did for me what I could not have done for myself.

The Journey of Recovery

July 10

Reflections on Anniversary Month

The Miracle

I regained presence of time and space overlooking a breathtaking Long Island Sound. It was a beautiful summer day. The universe had spared no splendor. The sun's reflection on the calm water shot rays of brilliant color across the sky. I was in the midst of experiencing a miracle; that which defies logical explanation.

It had never occurred to me to give up my way of life, this only because I did not think it possible. Although I had experienced inner spiritual moments and messages, I considered them to be the rambling thoughts of a foolish mind. I had come to accept my excruciatingly meaningless existence as my lot in life.

There was no specific conscious thought or message that morning. It was as if I was a vessel and Divine Power stepped onto the bridge, threw the False Prophet overboard, took the helm and command of my life. I did not resist. I went along with his chosen course.

As a result of letting go of my self-will and trusting in a Power Greater Than Myself, within hours this all-powerful force had taken me from darkness to light, from captivity to liberation. I am grateful for the surrender that came from somewhere within me on that unforgettable morning. I was never to be the same again.

The spiritual and the logical find themselves at odds in defining the origins of a miracle.

July 11

Reflections on Anniversary Month

A New Way of Life

I had grown accustomed to waking up unaware of the previous night's charades, having to sift through my mind's memories for clues and often accepting an unknown reality only known by those who'd been in my presence.

On this first morning of an unlikely journey, I woke up, looked around at the unfamiliar surroundings, and was unsure of the convoluted events that had brought me here. It all seemed surreal. Had I committed myself to a new way of life?

I was in a place where the broken sought redemption from their sins, solitude from the chaos of their disease, and direction toward rebirth, a fresh start from a punishing life. Surely, this must be a holy place, for it would take an act of providence to enlighten this weary lot to a path of recovery.

I experienced fear, excitement, hope, and an unfamiliar calm. I felt I was in the right place, yet I was apprehensive about the future. I was a sponge to this experience, welcoming any guidance to help me build a robust life.

Hope had taken root.

July 12

Reflections on Anniversary Month

The Three Wise Men

In previous half-hearted attempts at change, desire alone proved futile because it lacked sustenance. As a result, each attempt resulted in no lasting permanence. This time, I was willing to consider a new way of being, but only to resolve my troubles. Little did I know that I was about to embark on a journey that would offer more than my mind could comprehend.

To that end, the Universe placed three wise men in my life who had traveled a familiar path of peaks and valleys. They laid out a path for my ongoing, sustainable sobriety, its simplicity intrigued me.

A Higher Power tasked these imperfect servants with delivering a message of hope that touched my spirit and transformed my understanding of myself, others, and the world. I saw something in them that I longed to find within me.

July 13

Reflections on Anniversary Month

A Voice Cuts its Power

If I wanted to be different from what I had become, I would have to find another way of being.

I was careful to avoid people, places, and harmful thought patterns from my past. To avoid triggering old behaviors, I limited my exposure to negative influences and places I didn't need to be. I wanted to protect my recovery at all costs. There was no going back.

My delusional mind missed the drama of the past. It involuntarily created delusional scenarios that taunted my peace with doubt, jealousy, or resentment. These emotions threatened my emotional well-being. Any time spent in isolation added to the intensity of my discomfort.

Intrusive thoughts or disturbing feelings required immediate deflation. I could share my experiences in a twelve step meeting and give them a voice.

As challenging as it was at first, picking up what felt like a hundred-pound telephone and calling a recovering friend or someone in my circle of support helped me articulate my discomfort. Prayer provided comfort, even though my belief in a Higher Power was still growing.

It is essential to allow delusion a voice and thus weaken its power. The loving voice of another, or a moment of prayer, soothes or eliminates an unwelcome thought or feeling, and serenity can be temporarily restored.

The Journey of Recovery

July 14

Reflections on Anniversary Month

The First Three

I Can't!   *He Can!*   *I think I'll Let Him!*

Through instant gratification we seek a state of mind that provides only fleeting moments of happiness. Such is the imperfect nature of the human race. To some extent, we all suffer from a malady of the spirit, ranging from mild displeasure to severe disruption.

Alone, I could not untangle the web of deceit that had overpowered my limited moral virtues. Progress began when I became willing to look in the mirror and admit personal defeat. *I Can't!*

I met a group of people undergoing spiritual recovery that undoubtedly relieved their dis-ease. They had adapted a manner of living that allowed for a God of their understanding to enter their lives. I was out of answers and came to believe that what they had found could work for me. I joined their solution.

He can!

I realized maintaining sobriety was beyond human recourse. Through an ever-growing, ever-changing relationship with my Higher Power, I aligned my will with his and allowed his guidance.

I Think I'll Let Him!

In the First Three we find relief from a malady that has plagued our lives. The amount of effort we put into the process will determine the outcome of our recovery.

July 15

Reflections on Anniversary Month

Willingness Honesty Open-Mindedness

The universe's timely intervention interrupted my spiritual bankruptcy and restored me to sanity—but only because I became Willing to engage its guidance.

I didn't sign a binding contract, make a blood pact, or give up my power of thought or opinion, I simply removed the cotton from my ears and gave myself the opportunity to listen, to learn, to become teachable once more.

I became honest with myself by admitting the powerlessness of that which I could not control and honest in sharing that which I had kept hidden for fear of judgment, misunderstanding, or social retribution. I became Open-Minded to considering a Higher Power of my choosing that promised to provide an alternative to my spiritual imprisonment.

Shortly after beginning the work of the First Three, Willingness, Honesty and Open-Mindedness slowly spread from the classroom of my spiritual kindergarten, permeating all facets of my life; providing substance to the previously ignorant clatter of my mind and hope to my broken spirit.

July 16

Reflections on Anniversary Month

A Good Guy

It was a tremendous weight off my shoulders to understand my difficulties weren't due to being a "bad guy," but that I was a "good guy" suffering from a mental, physical, emotional and spiritual dis-ease. There was a solution, and it lay in developing and practicing a set of spiritual principles.

In my early recovery, I lacked the understanding of what "spiritual" truly meant. What did sink in was that I was not a bad person, and there was an answer to my chronic dilemma.

For years, I carried negative, hurtful labels as collateral damage of my self-centered character. So much so that, in despair, I believed myself hopeless. My rebirth gave me an opportunity for redemption. I was neither bad nor hopeless.

I was optimistically curious about what was to come and committed to embracing and holding on to this new version of myself— a Good Guy.

July 17

Reflections on Anniversary Month

Recovery Brings Awareness

With recovery came awareness. My daily choice of reality, not escapism, is fueled by my adherence to fundamental spiritual principles.

When I become aware of the return of self-centeredness, I take action or it will become an increasingly disruptive force. It manifests as inner turmoil and spills over into other areas of my life. Intolerance and unforgiveness obscures the spiritual solution, leading to mental and emotional chaos.

With awareness comes the duty to take action or, in certain situations, to do nothing at all. When I choose the mental solution, I am often conflicted. When I opt for the spiritual solution, I am rewarded with emotional clarity.

July 18

Reflections on Anniversary Month

We Can!

Mental, physical, or emotional suffering isolates us from the mainstream, and We retreat inward. During these times, We become disconnected from others and our spiritual source, and the light of hope becomes dim.

Alone, I am powerless to overcome my despair. I am rewarded with emotional clarity when I opt for the spiritual solution.

For so long, I had adapted to inner isolation. I found it challenging to be vulnerable and share my pain, but the other choice offered nothing—leaving me barren.

In joining the We, I shed my uniqueness and witnessed the overcoming of brokenness. We share the same spiritual purpose; a common bond of survival. "The We" ends our individual isolation as We become purposeful in each other's lives.

That which I alone could not, together We can!

July 19

Reflections on Anniversary Month

Showing Up

I found a place where my loneliness could rest. There were many days I was tempted to stay home and watch a ball game or avoid the recovery meeting because of exhaustion, but I rarely missed them. Showing up is half the battle.

Missing in action was a trait of my past. I had stopped showing up for life. I lacked discipline and courage. There had always been a part of me that wanted to show responsibility, but what little I showed was inconsistent. In this new way of living, I had to leave behind and improve upon all aspects of my past, starting with showing up.

After a day filled with perplexing life issues and human challenges, I found camaraderie and fellowship with my newfound friends. We shared our challenges, identified with each other, felt heard, supported, and understood. In our spiritual practice, we found a common solution.

For my presence I was rewarded with renewed hope and energy to continue this journey for another day. Each day I showed up, the guidance of a Higher Power reinforced the importance of my recovery, through the words and actions of this new family. I developed the discipline to show up for my spiritual treatment and in turn found myself showing up for life.

July 20

Reflections on Anniversary Month

Taking Suggestions

One day, for no particular reason, I felt bored with my new life, and the pink cloud I had been riding for months became transparent. As suggested, I shared about it with the group to lessen its power.

It was suggested that whenever I feel disappointed, it is a signal that I need to take a recovery-based action. When I take inventory, I eventually find something missing in my process; whether it is returning to a prayer ritual, making an overdue phone call, becoming more consistent with meeting attendance, or increasing service to my group or to another. Only through action do I regain my balance.

It was suggested that I seek connection with a Higher Power upon waking, thanking "God" for another day, and when laying my head on the pillow at night, thanking "God" for another day being sober. I did not believe in "God," but as with many other suggestions, I did it anyway. In a short time, I became comfortable with this first introduction to prayer. Even with limited but consistent dialogue/prayer, I was unknowingly being led to my own personal concept of a Higher Power.

This became a morning and evening ritual that continues to this day. It was by taking suggestions from the We that I found the spiritual solution.

"God" speaks through people!

July 21

Reflections on Anniversary Month

Problems Become Situations

Music blared, people laughed, a place where people left the world's problems at the door. I felt welcomed and understood. The spirits contributed to everyone's good mood and false sense of well-being. This had become my comfort zone, a place to escape responsibility through fantasy. I regularly overstayed my welcome. When I walked out, I found my problems had grown exponentially, my debts had increased, and I had left another piece of my soul behind.

The sixty-minute recovery meeting replaced the long nights of gratuitous mayhem. In these meetings, I check my worries at the door and am greeted with genuine joy. The power of the spirit is felt and shared. Our interactions are authentic. When I walk out the door, my problems have become situations with spiritual solutions, and hope floods my soul.

Acceptance of reality took the place of delusional escape.

July 22

Reflections on Anniversary Month

The Serenity Prayer

God grant me the Serenity to accept the things I cannot change; Courage to change the things I can; and Wisdom to know the difference.

I learned a number of Catholic prayers as a child, but I have long since forgotten them because none of them held much meaning to me.

When I began my journey of recovery, I was not too enthusiastic about learning another prayer; I thought my problems were beyond the help of worship. I wanted a practical solution. That is when I came across the Serenity Prayer. It hung on the walls of the rooms where I received my daily spiritual dose and we said it in unison at the end of each meeting. Initially, I paid little attention to it.

When the testy crises of early recovery tested my resilience, it was suggested I recite this prayer to soothe my displeasure. I gave it a try.

When I felt uneasy, I repeated it over and over and found that it interrupted and redirected intrusive, destabilizing thoughts. It became a tool to help me deflect negativity and doubt. I credit the Serenity Prayer with opening the door through which a Higher Power was to enter my life.

July 23

Reflections on Anniversary Month

The Mentor

"When the student is ready the teacher will appear." Lao Tzu

Along the way, I have benefited from many teachers and numerous teachable moments. I continue to be grateful for the daily lessons in life's classroom.

One mentor has been by my side since the beginning of my journey and whose experience, strength, and hope have touched me deeply. Through his actions, he models a way of being that I aspire to live. Through his words, he brings comfort and direction to my complex challenges. His trust in "God" has influenced me to develop a meaningful relationship with a power greater than myself. As a fallible man, he demonstrates accountability for his actions, humility in his failings, and forgiveness for his imperfections.

My mentor has been a beacon of light, guiding me through my darkest moments. If there were no teachers, how would I learn life's lessons?

July 24

Reflections on Anniversary Month

Spiritual Ways

I was clueless about spiritual ways, afraid that I might not find this illusory Higher Power that everyone talked about and that was supposed to be the only source of treatment for my illness. I was not one for patience, and patience was required, for our Higher Power reveals itself only through our creating honest intention and open-mindedness to its influence.

This force is within all of us. It is present in all our thoughts, in all our actions, in every breath we take. It is life itself. Yet it remains a mystery to our consciousness unless we actively seek it. After many years of relying on the mind for answers to my situations, it grew stronger, and in its dominance, it silenced the voice of the spirit—the voice of my Higher Power.

I dedicated myself to cultivating spiritual awareness in order to deepen my spiritual journey. I began by demonstrating pure intention and desire by becoming open to its existence within me through prayer; communicating with my Higher Power, and meditation; listening for my Higher Power.

The mind interferes with this process because it feels threatened by a force it doesn't understand. With daily persistence, continued faith and patience, small glimpses of insight revealed themselves in the form of Spirit Conscious; suddenly one day I felt a warm feeling from deep within, accompanied by a thought that "everything was going to be okay." I had made contact and was on my way to developing a relationship with my concept of a Higher Power that would restore me to sanity.

July 25

Reflections on Anniversary Month

Fake It Until You Make It

When we find the courage to surrender the unsuccessful methods we've used to remedy or escape our overwhelming lives, we arrive at early recovery. We're angry with the world, and the world is angry with us. We don't feel like we belong, and the world doesn't seem interested in welcoming us back. These are natural responses to abnormal situations.

The starting point was the most challenging. It was suggested I "Fake it Until I Make it." I began by pretending I was not angry or resentful. A fake smile replaced an irritated frown. The world could not tell if I was faking. It saw my smile and smiled back.

I faked a kind word when I felt it necessary. A kind word prompts a kind response and when it did not respond, at least it ceased to utter something under its breath. This was progress.

Slowly, the world embraced this kinder me. What was fake at first became my natural way of being, and before I knew it, my smiles and kind words were genuine.

The world became more welcoming and my desire to rejoin the human race grew. Old thoughts and ways of being faded.

July 26

Reflections on Anniversary Month

Removing the Blocks

I severed ties with old behaviors, but for my prayers to be answered, some large boulders blocking the light of my soul had to be removed. These obstacles to inner peace required immediate attention, lest the candle of hope be extinguished, and I turn back with no hope of returning.

Earthly concerns, left unattended, get in the way of spiritual growth. I had an IRS debt to settle, need for a long overdue physical exam, to show accountability to my creditors, assume my role as a responsible employer, and most importantly, show consistency, reliability, and presence for my most important role of being a loving father to my son.

With each block removed, my hope, determination, self-worth, and my trust in a Higher Power grew. I began to experience an unexplainable inner calm, and hope began to sprout in barren fields that had previously produced only doubt and fear.

July 27

Reflections on Anniversary Month

One Day at a Time

But how is it possible to socialize, go to a ball game, celebrate holidays, attend a wedding, or drown my sorrows without including a false prophet? My new wise companions, always prepared with a simple answer to my seemingly complicated questions, suggested that I try to live "One Day at a Time."

In the past, whenever another debacle was about to unfold, even though it would undoubtedly interfere with my responsibilities, I would override any rational thought with, "Why worry about tomorrow? I'll deal with it when it comes." It appears I have been living "One Day at a Time" for most of my adult life.

Recovery life came with a guarantee—one that I did not want to claim: "If I am not fully satisfied, my misery will be returned to me, in its entirety." I tricked my mind with the concept of "One day at a time," but I understood that this was different from the insincere attempts of the past, this was not an empty promise, it was to be a new, continuous, permanent way of living.

I willingly pledge to live my remaining days sober, "One Day at a Time."

July 28

Reflections on Anniversary Month

Abstinence – Sobriety

Through mental, emotional, behavioral, and spiritual flexibility, I showed resilience in maintaining abstinence from chemical and behavioral obsessions. This significantly improved my quality of life, but abstinence is not to be confused with sobriety, which would arrive sometime later.

Although I no longer suffered from crippling obsessions, my thinking needed vast improvement. Years of grandiosity, arrogance, and self-centeredness require spiritual treatment.

My sobriety emerged when I connected with the universe in gratitude, forgave past hurts, prioritized others, and relinquished self-centeredness.

The natural progression from Abstinence to Sobriety occurred naturally through incorporating moral principles into my life, resulting in a notable progression in my humility, modesty, and selflessness.

July 29

Reflections on Anniversary Month

From Victim to Survivor

Had I seized the moment, the conditions for earthly prestige and financial success were of my choosing. I wasted every opportunity and fell into a deep well of self-pity. For convenience, I assumed the role of victim, and for a time, this manipulative deception was successful. Eventually, what had been a role became my reality. I came to accept that the world needs its "losers" as well.

Only days removed from my last debacle and with sparse spiritual treatment, I could already see the insanity of my old thinking. Recovery held no room for victimization. I was to take responsibility for my actions, reach out for help in the form of human or spiritual guidance, and turn the page. I was blessed with a re-do, a fresh start. I was a survivor.

I have gained a new perspective on the circumstances of my life. Although "the victim" is lurking for an opportunity to disturb my peace, as long as I live under the protection provided within the confines of my spiritual practice, it will not succeed.

The overcoming of my obsessions through a spiritual solution to my dis-ease transformed me from a hopeless victim into an unwavering survivor.

July 30

Reflections on Anniversary Month

Invite Love

We are born with pure, innocent love, free from the burdens of judgment, doubt, or expectation. As infants, giving and receiving love was as natural as our shallow breathing or the transparency of our emotions.

How, then, did my pure spirit become so corrupted that I succumbed to confusion and self-loathing? The complexities of living in an impure world brought it about.

The transformation of self-hatred to self-love and confusion to clarity was achieved through the process of recovery. It allowed me the insight to step back and retreat to a place of sacred neutrality, careful not to place blame on myself, others, or the circumstances that contributed to the derailment of my original innocence.

Through spiritual practice, the powers at work in our lives take us on a remarkable journey that remains a mystery to all of us. By willingly and intentionally giving love and allowing myself to be loved, I have turned my back on self-hatred, found continual relief from the unnatural trappings of life's burdens, and live in serenity.

When we give love, We invite love!

July 31

Reflections on Anniversary Month

The Solution

I moved away from self-reliance and allowed for guidance from a spiritual power. In doing so, I found a solution to my addiction, anger, resentment, self-pity, jealousy, and other maladaptive behaviors and states of mind. As part of my humanity, imperfections and delusions remain in part, but now with a diminished ability to disturb my serenity.

Through what can only be described as a moment of divine intervention, I escaped captivity. I found the light. Though it was blinding and uncomfortable at first, I sensed I could eventually adapt. The one thing I was sure of was that I did not want to return to the dark misery of my recent past.

Being inquisitive and naturally skeptical, I expanded my spiritual inquiry through education, working with others, and exploring other spiritual methods. I found a common theme; that of embracing an Unseen Spirit who brings divine meaning to earthly existence.

The 12 Step meetings I participate in started me on this journey and will always be at the center of my life. It's where I find my higher purpose of giving to others what has been so freely given to me. Yet, my solution lies in a Higher Power that captains my life from the rough waters of earthly being to the calm seas of divinity.

I have found my Truth. It is no longer bathed in the innocence and grandeur of my boyhood dreams. Today, my Truth is found in knowing that one day I will come to rest in a place of peaceful serenity.

August 1

The Journey of Recovery

The Spiritual Pilgrimage of the Rainbow

During the heaviest downpours of thunder and lightning, with no shelter in sight, in fear and desperation, we turned to a God we did not believe in and bartered a life of devotion in exchange for our survival.

The storm's end brought old negative patterns and behaviors to a halt and gave way to blue skies and the majestic, colorful wonders of a rainbow. We experienced relief, clarity, hope, and gratitude that the seemingly never-ending tempest had passed.

We gracefully accepted protection and entered into communion with our personal guardian, who admonished us to follow the Spiritual Pilgrimage of the Rainbow. In this way, we would avoid or find protection from all inclement weather that we may encounter.

We have been given the simple task of obedience to basic moral principles, and in return we have been promised His protection. Each day we freely choose our path; to live our will into the perilous unknown, or to abide by our agreement and follow His guidance on the Spiritual Pilgrimage of the Rainbow.

August 2

The Principle of Acceptance

Not to accept reality is to row against the current. It is to deny the Truth. Without acceptance of what is, it will be difficult to move on to the remaining principles.

We may have difficulty with this principle if we believe acceptance means taking a slap on the cheek with no reaction. It means no such thing. It means acknowledging our reality and our power to take whatever action deemed appropriate to bring about change in any situation that we feel is harmful to our mental, emotional, or physical well-being.

We accept our present circumstances as they are and people as they are. Their faults are our faults. Acceptance restrains us from being reactionary. We accept the fallibility of being human. In our humility, we do not project expectations but accept our limitations. All the while, we strive to be our best selves.

Acceptance, like all principles, requires desire, understanding, and commitment. It requires daily vigilance and practice. It is a slow process in which we eventually intuitively know that the situation we are experiencing, whether pleasant or not, is uniquely ours. As such, and with no other reasonable option, we welcome it into our lives.

The principle of acceptance promotes serenity for us, for them, and for the world.

August 3

The Principles of Faith and Hope

Without faith, there is no hope.

Accepting a situation does not mean that I don't want to create change. It simply means I accept the reality of its existence.

I used to be full of wishful thinking. I had fantasies of prestige, power, and possessions. Few of my unrealistic desires ever came true. My misplaced priorities lacked drive and ambition. I lacked faith and hope. Living at the level of the mind, I was limited to reliance on self.

Faith is the fuel that ignites motivation for action. With faith, I enter communion with the Divine Power and set out to achieve my previously illusory goals. Instead of relying on self, I allow the Divine Mind to guide me.

Hope is an optimistic expectation supported by intention and action. I believe and act as if success is guaranteed. Success is found on the journey, not on the outcome.

Self-guidance failed me, so I followed Good Orderly Direction. My Higher Power's Will was not for my grandiose wishful thinking instead; He led me to modest but enlightening spiritual heights.

August 4

The Principle Honesty

An honest inventory will reveal the assets and liabilities of our past behavior. Only after a thorough examination can we move forward on our spiritual journey.

The best way to do this is to put our inventory on paper. It brings our past to life and gives us a realistic view of the roads we have traveled. It takes courage to go into the dark corners of our minds and bring to light the irreversible damage we have done to others and ourselves. We gain this courage because we have begun practicing the preceding principles.

Once we have completed our inventory, we will share it with someone who has themselves experienced a spiritual awakening as a result of this process. An honest reflection with another makes it possible for our past to see the light.

This process cleanses us of the accumulated secrets and shame from our past wrongdoings. We feel lighter, freer, and ready for the next challenge to arise as we travel on our journey to spiritual enlightenment.

August 5

Principle of Patience

After reviewing our inventory, we became aware of our defects of character. We humbly acknowledge that in order to grow as spiritual beings, we must change our attitude and treatment of ourselves and of others. Having awareness and a sincere desire for growth is all we need to get started with this task.

One of our defects is a demand for what we want, when we want it. This selfish, self-centered attitude was at our core. Throughout this process, we must practice Patience. Change does not come overnight. It will require daily practice and steady vigilance for progress to be noted.

We need to grow our modesty and accept our humanness. To accept that we do not have the answers and that alone, we are doomed. This one-of-a-kind opportunity for growth warrants our appreciation.

Patience is an essential ingredient of humility.

August 6

Principle of Humility

For those of us who for so long relied only on ourselves for all the answers, it will be humbling to sit with our Higher Power, acknowledge our flawed past and ask for guidance.

We enter into communion with the Unseen Spirit and request that His Will for us be revealed. We can do this by finding moments of quiet conscious communication.

This is not as exorbitant a task as it may appear. With patience and humility, in a short time, the result of our efforts will bloom, and a new character will reveal itself to us and to those engaged in our lives.

We would do well surrounding ourselves with strong, healthy, spiritually evolved individuals. They may be of help in keeping our shortcomings in check. Their suggestions offer alternatives to the situations and dysfunctions we've faced in the past.

With patience and humility and with the help of our fellows and our Higher Power, our past's dark, negative character will fade, giving way to a bright, selfless, positive Being.

August 7

Discipline Yields Results

Discipline is a commitment to a predictable but uncertain outcome.

Discipline is required when we seek to change the course of our lives. As we begin to live new emotional, physical and spiritual routines, our conditioned mind struggles with the change, preferring to maintain the status quo. Through practice, the mind can be reconditioned to adopt new ways of thinking and living.

In the past, we experienced our negativity growing to destructive proportions. A pessimistic chill extinguished the flame of our spirits, leaving us in the dark. The way out is to adopt and live by spiritual principles.

Only with Discipline will we implement, embrace and adhere to these principles. In doing so, the glow of optimism will relight our wick and brighten our spirit, and our uncertain outcomes will inherit predictable results.

August 8

Living the Principles

We Accepted that our way of life was not working for us. We needed to change and grow spiritually.

Faith and hope led us to believe we could find peace and serenity by learning and practicing spiritual principles.

We found the courage to take a thorough inventory and honestly share our dark past.

Through patience and humility, we began to recognize and overcome our shortcomings.

We became disciplined in practicing spiritual principles in all our affairs.

As a result of practicing spiritual principles, our self-seeking has given way to selflessness.

By allowing ourselves to be guided by the Spiritual Source, we have found peace and serenity!

Living by spiritual principles gives our journey meaning, purpose, and direction.

August 9

Acceptance is a Process

Acceptance is a process, not an event. The starting point is to see reality and accept it as Truth. It happened; therefore it is. Tolerating, trying to understand, forgetting, or holding resentment is not acceptance.

Practicing simple acceptance is to experience a rainy day as a necessity for flowers to bloom and rivers to flow. Still, there have been times when rain has caused us inconvenience and resentment. Acceptance is a process, not an event.

Experiences of regret, anguish, and sorrow require a more complex form of acceptance. Only through our acceptance of loss will we end periods of grief. Acceptance is a process, not an event.

Acceptance may trigger action or allow for being. But accept we must. Denial is to negate existence itself. Only when we accept circumstances for their Truth, be they of joy or hurt, will we live in reality.

August 10

A Privileged Life

While sitting on a crowded train, my mind was distracted by a moment of clarity. I felt a sudden awareness of my privileged life.

I'm too busy feeling sorry for myself instead of assuming that the only hell I've experienced is of my making. Hastily interrupting or tuning out the suffering of others in favor of my salvation.

These welcome insights into self-awareness result from being open, if only for brief moments, to detach from the self-consumed notion of my physical presence and allow my spiritual inner self to have a voice.

I thank you, Great Unseen Friend, for all the favors you have bestowed upon me, and with deep sorrow, I apologize for wasting so much of your light. I pray that by heeding your Guidance and Will for me, the time remaining in my sentient life may be used for the benefit of others.

August 11

Defective Traits

If we commit ourselves to living a spiritually guided life, we will recognize our progress in due course. Progress brought awareness of my many defective traits. The greater the progress, the higher the bar of expectation and the greater the personal scrutiny.

Last year's challenges helped me identify behaviors and shortcomings that needed improvement in the coming year. Sometimes it feels like I know a little less each year. The less I "know" on the level of the mind is actually an indication that I have progressed on the path to pure spiritual knowledge.

Recognizing negative traits and maintaining constant vigilance over them is the way to progress. Only through this process can I strengthen my character. A compassionate character is one that moves away from self-will and self-gratification and toward an increased motivation to be of service to others.

August 12

The Power of Faith

Faith is the acceptance of Divine Direction—a path that leads to love and inner peace.

Without faith, life becomes a journey through a desert of delusion. In its absence, I am led by the illusions of the mind, ruled by the ego.

Guided by ego-driven desires, I place myself at the center of the universe, seeking only to satisfy my selfish, materialistic cravings.

Faith teaches me to cherish others; ego compels me to cherish only myself.

Faith opens my heart to receive love from others; ego isolates me and leaves me alone.

The choice is clear: Live without faith—aimless and without purpose. Or choose a life of faith—directed, selfless, and grounded in meaningful service.

August 13

A Great Gift

My pain has become my Great Gift.

Every time I've reached a breaking point, the light of the Spirit, when sought, has shone through me. It is this light that guides my path.

My daily, permanent relationship with this Limitless Power brightens my joys and soothes my sorrows. I know of no other effective way to survive moments of emotional despair.

This enlightening power is available to us all in calm, and storm. It is often my only option for sanity. My Great Gift has become the door through which I've walked to welcome and embrace the Spirit of the Universe.

August 14

Triggering Aftershocks

When our mental torment became too great, we encountered a chemical solution and our symptoms were temporarily relieved. The side effects became worse than the original agony and caused us irreversible mental anguish.

Even in recovery, when distress persists—however infrequently—it signals that echoes of that torment still linger, triggering aftershocks. This is a gentle reminder that we have not yet fully disengaged from the root causes of our dis-ease.

Peace will elude us as long as malice lingers. To experience true serenity, we must fully detach from the pain we hold on to. But even when our minds, out of selfishness, try to justify clinging to what still causes us hurt, we are no longer prisoners of that pain. Restored to sanity, we now stand at a crossroads—our spirit, having grown in Truth, empowers us to choose differently.

We accept our choice, and through much prayer, our symptoms are lightened. But only through an act of courage will they be eliminated and we will come to know peace.

August 15

Not Today!

On this morning's run, I faced a steep climb. I have run up this hill many times before, but on this day, about halfway up, my mind decided that I should slow down to a walk. It challenged my resolve.

With every stride, I felt a burn in my quads, my heart rate increased, and I questioned my resilience. My mind took advantage of my struggle and fired off a series of negative thoughts, and I wanted to give in to its will. Just then, a voice from within whispered, *"Not Today!"* I used *"Not Today"* as a positive mantra to disarm negative thinking and carry me to the top.

So often, in other areas of my life, I give in to the will of my mind. When I do, I am taking the easy way out, bypassing discipline, seeking immediate gratification, buying into delusional thinking, or attempting to avoid physical or emotional discomfort.

To detach from the negativity that arises from a mind that often impedes progress, interferes with decision-making, or minimizes my resolve, I will listen for inner spiritual guidance and heed its mantra: *"Not Today!"*

August 16

Forever Grateful

Welcoming another to our fellowship is an amazing gift to ourselves and the universe. The miracle is that they, like us, have found the courage to surrender. We are not of the surrendering type.

Each of us arrived at spiritual recovery after having had different experiences and traveling different routes. The one thing we all have in common, which can only be truly understood by another who has walked the same path, is the gut-wrenching pain we felt just before that moment of surrender.

We found the courage to let go of what had once been our solution, our best friend, our confidant, our higher power. Our pain became our greatest blessing and we are Forever Grateful.

August 17

Spirit Needs Company

To become whole, we must first enter into and maintain a relationship with a God of our understanding. The space within, where emptiness resides, will then be filled with His grace.

We are on our way, but only halfway to our intended purpose, for we cannot fully rejoice in this spiritual experience unless we share it. We are to elicit grace from our spiritual practice and live it in all our affairs.

When on the open road or stuck in traffic
We allow for spirit's calm!

When we're confident and when we're fearful
We allow for spirit's calm!

When we're serene and when we're disturbed
We allow for spirit's calm!

Through the living and sharing of our Higher Power's grace, others are encouraged. Spirit gains momentum and creates community, and our world becomes a better place.

Spirits Needs Company!

August 18

Happiness and Suffering

In the morning, I ask my Spiritual Guide to guide my day. In the evening, I take inventory of my actions. In the past, I categorized good days as those when life went my way and bad days as those that did not unfold as I wished.

With the introduction to Spiritual Principles came a new way of perceiving each experience—one that does not allow for me to judge my days, months, or years. Regardless of my selfish interpretation, each day is a perfect day. Perhaps not to my liking, but a loving Universal Guide routinely and without fail provides all the elements necessary for our world to function in perfect order.

Let each day be filled with gratitude for the many blessings this journey has given us. Our gratitude list should include Happiness and Suffering, for they are the bookends of our human experience.

We can choose how we interpret each day; with an eye of defeatism or with a vision of gratitude. Our choice will determine the type of energy we carry and directly affect our outlook on life.

August 19

Honor Our Loyalty

Twelve Step programs encourage a relationship with a God of our understanding, for that is the primary purpose of the 12 Steps. Their design is to shift our focus from self-centeredness to selflessness.

Recovery is best achieved as part of a "we" because as an "I," we lack resolve. Through the fellowship of the Spirit we are reminded of who we were, how far we've come, but also that we are vulnerable to a dormant disease. We are recovered but not cured.

We carry the message and practice the principles in all our affairs, for we are the ones to whom a newcomer looks for guidance. We, too, have learned from others of spiritual practice.

Through service, we Honor Our Loyalty to a Higher Power and the recovery program, ensuring that the tradition continues for those who have not yet found the courage to walk through our open doors.

August 20

The Children

We often speak of our children. Although we gave birth to them, they are by no means ours. They are children of our shared Father, the Eternal Heart.

When they do "good," it is their accomplishment, their effort, of which we can be proud, but in no way do we take credit. For if we took credit for the "good," we would also have to take blame for their "bad." Their "bad" choices sadden us, but we must not take on their burdens. How else will they learn? We should help, but we cannot enable.

We patiently watch, love, and pray, but also let go and allow their process to unfold. While in no way minimizing our role as parents, I find it necessary to remain mindful that they, too, have a Higher Power who is attentively guiding their journey.

August 21

The Temple Of The Spiritual Heart

During difficult emotional times, when I feel suffocated by fear, resentment and self-pity, I seek refuge from these great delusions of the mind. We need not react punitively against ourselves or others when circumstances cause mental upset, for this can add to our suffering. We will find wisdom in allowing time for reflection.

We can find solace in having a ritual where our Spirit can shelter from inclement sorrow, a place where we can lay down our burdens and rest. This place of safety is not a place at all, but a state of calm brought about by spiritual action. There is no one way to practice.

I take refuge in the temple of the spiritual heart. I enter into communion with my Higher Power through meditation and then lay my sadness at His feet.

With my mind still, I can listen for the loving guidance of the inner spirit. Not all disturbances can be irrevocably resolved through the spiritual process, but we leave the Temple of the Spiritual Heart equipped with a calm perspective and a spiritual alternative.

August 22

Crisis and Conflict

Our mind registers all our thoughts, attitudes, and perceptions. When we are calm, our ideas become clear, enabling us to find answers. Cycles and repetition define life, including its challenges. With realistic understanding, we find practical solutions.

Finding a solution to conflict at the level of the mind is more complex. In crisis mode our thoughts become confused and we become apathetic or negative. We lack insight and our reactions to circumstances often create more confusion than clarity. Crisis and conflict are inevitable. The level of intensity and manageability are dependent on our spiritual condition.

By practicing the spiritual principles of mindfulness, acceptance, faith, courage, patience, and humility, we achieve higher levels of spiritual well-being and are more likely to avert crisis or conflict.

The solution to unavoidable human challenges, become clear to a serene mind.

August 23

Restoring Spiritual Order

Whether in our daily personal commitments, work obligations, or our recovery, creating order through prioritization, provides purpose and discipline from a life run riot.

In my previous life, I was the only priority. I lived with unidirectional goals, with self-seeking in the realm, gasping for survival from a spiritually impoverished lifestyle. Once in recovery, I found the need to restore inner spiritual order by prioritizing my spiritual practice.

Whether I'm with family, friends, at work, or at leisure, I all times experience the presence of my Spiritual Guide. I incorporate spiritual practice into every part of my life. Once in recovery, I found the need to restore inner spiritual order by prioritizing my spiritual connection—this became the root from which all other areas of my life would grow.

If we accept the guidance of our Spiritual Guide, we will live a recovered, disciplined, and richly purposeful life.

August 24

Mind Body and Soul

Over time, I've gathered a wealth of valuable information to optimize ongoing mental, physical and spiritual well-being. Simple concepts and actions take little time out of my daily routine, but would improve the overall quality of my life. Yet, for the most part, this information sits in a dark corner of my brain, gathering dust.

Motivation for action comes only in moments of desperation, usually when I am experiencing physical, emotional, or spiritual discomfort. Abstaining from delusional thinking, drinking more water, developing a healthy diet, and devoting at least 30 minutes to daily exercise help to clear an inflamed body; regular meditation keeps me connected to the spiritual realm.

Caring for mental, physical, and spiritual well-being is how we honor our temple—our body. To ignore one is to ignore them all. The path to happiness is through our efforts to respectfully care for ourselves. We must use the information that is so readily available to us for the purpose of peaceful longevity of Mind, Body, and Soul.

August 25

Denial

To overcome Denial, we accept Truth.

Denial is a defense mechanism that protects us from imminent danger. It is triggered on rare occasions and for short periods. When we sense imminent danger, our Denial pulls the trigger for quick action and saves us from danger.

Denial can be misused by the mind to justify, avoid, or protect us from emotional pain. In these situations, Denial activates maladaptive behaviors that it then puts on hold for later reckoning, delaying the inevitable and causing irreparable damage to our character. It can be so powerful that, if left untreated, we live a lifetime in a state of Denial.

Through enhancing our spiritual knowledge, we gain insight and become less susceptible to delusional states of mind. With spiritual practice, our honesty spares us Denial. We no longer depend on justification because we live in Truth.

August 26

Making the Bed

My mother had a habit of making the bed right after she got up, and she tried to persuade me to do the same. I could not understand the importance of this ritual. I was just going to mess it up later that night anyway! What was the point? Who would know? Besides my mother, who cared if my bed was made?

As I grew older, I gave all the importance to what people saw of my outside. Hidden behind the curtain, my inside, was of little importance. As a result, I placed a great deal of importance on my outward appearance; fancy clothes, sharp haircut, shiny car, flashing money. All the while I was broken inside, I was living a lie.

As I began my journey of recovery and living by new principles, making my bed took on a different meaning. Today it is the first thing I do after my feet hit the ground. I care more about my inside than my outside.

I don't make a perfect bed. It's a work in progress. I don't live a perfect life, either. I, too, am a work in progress. My conversion began with small things, like making my bed. Today, my outside matches my inside. My focus is no longer on what others see. I know when my bed isn't made, and I know when I'm not living a principled life.

Although I don't live a perfect life, I am certainly a long way from living a lie.

August 27

Destiny

I do not believe that there is a master plan that predetermined my future. I've made my own choices and am ultimately responsible for my mistakes and successes.

Destiny is a personal choice to which only I can invite Divine Guidance. I can choose to be guided by self-will or I can choose to be guided by inner Spirit.

Self-will is arrogant and self-centered. It's primarily concerned with selfish needs, so that even charity serves a personal interest. My will is shaped by life experiences and clouded by the earthly need for physical and emotional survival.

Inner Spirit is as pure today as it was the day I was born, for Inner Spirit cannot be tainted. It carries a pure, unadulterated message from the Spirit of the Universe. Its primary concern is that I maintain a loving relationship with myself, with you, and with the world.

Although some defend the concept of a God of fate, I remain neutral toward such a view. I live by the belief that a life guided by the Inner Spirit learns from every willful choice.

Joy and suffering each have a meaning that only the spirit can decipher.

August 28

Divine Energy

Years before I experienced spiritual awareness, I felt an inexplicable energy when I visited places of worship. My rational mind would not allow for an understanding of the natural senses that could not be confirmed. Spiritual energy comes from the world of the supernatural. Words fail to explain it. It presents itself in the form of Divine Energy. I did not deny the power of religion, but I questioned the complexity of its rituals.

Spiritually, is the simple practice of intentional love for others through humility and surrender to a Higher Will that leads to tranquil well-being. Unity occurs when a group of individuals come together for spiritual purpose.

Tranquility and Unity are byproducts of Divine Energy. It must be fueled, or it is easily extinguished by the logic of a rational mind. Communing with others provides the fuel that keeps the guiding light of my Spirit bright.

August 29

Being Fully Present

When I'm taking a picture, I'm not fully present.

When I frivolously alter my consciousness with food, chemicals, or behaviors, I am not fully present.

When I'm lost in anger, resentment, jealousy, or self-pity, I am not fully present.

When I'm on social media, I am not fully present.

Why do I allow my mind to invest so much time in distraction? Because it's effortless.

Being fully present requires effort. In the moment, I must acknowledge my feelings and emotions and take responsibility for my actions.

I am too easily distracted by a dangling shiny object, which takes me out of the present moment and into mindless ambiguity.

Being present requires only physical existence.

Being fully present requires that I eliminate all mental intrusions that interrupt the honoring of the unique gift of the Spiritual Now.

August 30

Inevitable Softening

There are difficult people and situations in our lives that we cannot escape. We've tried to change them without success, but they resist our ways. Perhaps we should look at ourselves, past or present, at our own resistances, which help us empathize and understand them better. We may come to the solution that it is we who need to change our attitudes or perspectives.

By accepting our shared humanity without judgment, we can replace the frustrating impasse with a peaceful embrace of what was once unbearable.

With patience, time, and loving understanding, our change will have its effect. Unbeknownst to them, their guard will have lowered, and we will experience their inevitable softening.

The only way to motivate change in previously unchangeable people or circumstances is to change what we can control: our resistance, empathy, and compassion.

August 31

Restless Irritable and Discontent

As I looked at my garden this morning, I noticed it needed some attention. The dry summer and lack of watering had allowed the weeds to grow tall and invasive, but the flowers had withered.

How is it that the weeds grow without nourishment, and yet the flowers lose their enthusiasm? It is the same with my character defects. Without spiritual treatment, negative traits flourish, and suddenly, I begin to feel Restless, Irritable, and Discontent—at odds with people, places, and things. My grievances increase while my gratitude decreases. This dis-ease is dangerous for us in recovery because we can easily slip back into old addictive patterns, obsessions, or compulsions.

Just as daily care of our garden ensures an abundance of colorful flowers, consistency in our spiritual practice will induce our most virtuous qualities. Only with fervent devotion to spiritual principles in all areas of our lives will we minimize the weeds of our character, allowing our righteous traits to burst with color and keeping our garden of life serene and undisturbed.

September 1

The Piano

The old piano sits idle in the corner, wanting to provide sounds of cheer—wanting to fulfill its purpose of bringing joy to the world. It is relegated to stagnation. By itself, it cannot fulfill its potential.

Some of us live our whole lives without achieving our purpose. Like the piano, we alone lack such power. We become a revered instrument when guided by our Divine Master. Only in His trusting hands, playing His chosen tune, do we fulfill our human purpose and realize our full capacity. For only He has the ability to inspire the most sacred potential within us.

Of our own will, we, too, are an inert instrument. As an instrument of the Most High Spirit, living in the rhythm of God, we will assume our highest purpose.

September 2

The Interested Watcher

We tend to become attached to the circumstances of our existence, entangled in earthly dramas as we are. It is only when we break free from them we are able to encounter the serenity we seek.

Our soul's disease results from our attachment to the earthly emotional roller coaster. We experience sadness, but we are not our sadness, nor are we the event that caused the sadness. When we step back and become The Interested Watcher, we can observe sadness from a safe distance, rather than joining or assuming the emotion or situation.

We ought not to fight the disappointment we feel about a situation in our lives. Instead, we can embrace it, acknowledge it as uniquely ours, dance with it, and then let it go. Its memory will not be erased, but after going through this process, it will no longer consume us because we've made peace with it.

Spiritual progress, takes desire and practice; it is not a natural process. We break through old patterns and entanglements and from playing an active role in the dramas of our lives by stepping back from earthly attachments and becoming The Interested Watcher.

September 3

The Leopard

The Leopard cannot change its spots. In the same way, we cannot change our loving nature. Over the years, I have worked with many angry, resentful individuals, some institutionalized in prisons, psychiatric wards, or addiction rehabilitation centers, and not one of them has ever seemed to me to be devoid of compassion.

We are born a blank slate; our personality is then slowly shaped over time, by our various earthly experiences. Our negative traits originate as defense mechanisms, to ensure our emotional survival.

The spiritual path gently nudges us toward humble acceptance and surrender to the process of change. Spiritual conversion is perpetuated by the desire to escape our suffering, which is often the result of our negative actions.

In communion with our Higher Power, we feel safe to admit to Him and to ourselves the nature of our shortcomings. Our shame and guilt lessen once these are exposed. Releasing our past brings our compassion back into the light.

Although the leopard may not have the ability to remove its spots, we can change ours. But only if we develop the desire to submit to a Spiritual Conversion.

September 4

False Pride

When I offer my opinion as the solution, need to have the last word, correct another individual, or unnecessarily overreact to another's actions because I feel slighted, I am exhibiting false pride.

This is the nature of dis-ease; the relentless self-centered fear of being found out as not being good enough. I compensate for my perceived inferiority through arrogant, passive-aggressive displays of superiority.

I had tried to break through a brick wall by imposing my will. Tired and bloodied, I surrendered to humility. Arrogance was humbled as I accepted imperfection and let go of control.

Letting go of False Pride through the silence of humility is liberating. It gives the mind rest from vain preoccupations, distances me from the insatiable need for earthly approval, and brings me closer to the Great Reality. I've come to accept that all along I have been the only one in judgment of my Self.

September 5

Romancing The Thought

When our thoughts romanticize an old behavior, it is brought to life.

This can be positive if it's a productive thought. Otherwise, we must exercise caution. Often we forget the pain an experience brought us and allow for only the temporary pleasure of its initial effect.

In recovery, we must be careful not to entertain thoughts of past chemical, relational, emotional, or behavioral escapes. In moments of weakness, thoughts have the ability to trigger or set in motion irreversible actions that destroy our progress. These disturbing thoughts are more persistent when we are lonely, sad, or under emotional stress.

Hence the importance of daily care of our spiritual condition, the inner strength that holds our joy, gratitude, and sobriety together. When we stay spiritually fit, in times of emotional imbalance, when destabilizing thoughts come to life, we don't romanticize them—we allow the inner spirit to quietly bid them farewell.

September 6

No Cure!

A cure for the human condition would imply erasing all the wreckage and suffering of our past. There is no cure. If there were a cure, how would we benefit from life's lessons? Obstacles and situations are the weights with which we strengthen our character. It is in overcoming our obstacles that we increase our perseverance and our tolerance.

Every situation in our lives carries a message for our growth. In our pessimism about the human journey, we allow for hardship and self-pity.

We cultivate optimism when we welcome all experiences as opportunities for growth. The human condition is limited to time and space; our spiritual experience is unencumbered by pride or ego. Here we learn valuable character-building lessons.

Only through turbulent waters do we become strong swimmers, a cure would calm the seas of life and we would not be prepared for the rough currents to come.

September 7

Like a Wave

Each of us is given a vital role to play in the intricate process of earthly existence. Though crucial, our part is small; we cannot overstate our importance, yet we must accept our limitations.

We're like a wave that washes ashore, adding one more grain of sand to the shoreline, and then recedes back into the greater force, the ocean. It takes many waves and many tides to complete a beach; we'll have made our contribution.

Like the ocean, our lives are made up of calm waters and turbulent seas. The ocean is guided by the moon, we are guided by our mind. Both our mind and the moon are dependent on the supreme guidance of the Mighty Spirit of the Universe. Each wave, small or large, is a part of the ocean; each individual, regardless of ability, is a part of humanity.

Fighting the ocean currents is an unwinnable battle; just like going against the Will of Spirit brings exhaustion and suffering. We can choose to live our lives like a wave; accepting the guidance from the majestic ocean and taking pride in knowing that without our individual, seemingly insignificant grains of sand, the beach would not have come to be.

September 8

Awaken Spirit Consciousness

We are spiritual beings having a human experience.

Animals, plants, fish, insects, and humans all have a natural state of being and depend on the Divine Consciousness of the Universe for their survival.

Man has strayed from Higher Consciousness and has placed his dependency on the "developed" mind. We have come to be in a state of "doing." All other living organisms have remained faithful to Divine-Consciousness. The deer, the tree, and the whale are all in a constant state of "Being."

It is the human mind that is responsible for the conflict and destruction of our planet. All other organisms live in harmony and according to the Will of the Unseen Spiritual Source.

We can change the course of our destiny if we too, align our will with that of the Unseen Source. Individually, we may not be able to single-handedly bring about world peace, but we allow for spiritual principles to guide us we will awaken Spirit Consciousness and come to know inner peace.

September 9

The Leap of Faith

It seems an obvious choice to leave behind a punishing life and jump from the muddy fields where we are stuck, across the stream of malice, to the land of magnificent grass and blue skies where serenity dwells. In fact, it is not!

Often, we don't believe that serenity exists at all, much less for us. We are unable to see its magnificence, as darkness transforms into light only when in flight, revealing the beauty of the realm of Spiritual Awareness.

Only when I was exhausted by suffering did I take the leap. Still, it took an inexplicable moment of grace for me to push off. Once in the air, there was no going back.

The mystery remains as to why so many are unwilling to let go of their tortured lives. For those we pray that one day, perhaps today, they will take the Leap of Faith that will free them from their misery.

After suffering, it is possible to experience peace.

September 10

Our Unique Footprint

Life involves many responsibilities in our personal, social, and professional lives. I worry we may reach the end of our time without understanding who we are or what our purpose is. We become so preoccupied with checking off items on our life's to-do list that we lose our spontaneity.

Is our current path aligned with our truest, inner calling? Or are we tied to a career because it provides the income we need to meet our material needs? Do we wake up each morning excited about the day that awaits us? Or do we wake up each day with a knot in our stomach?

We must honor our family and social obligations, but we should also make compromises to accommodate precious time spent connecting with our true self. Our true self carries our Truth, our purpose for this journey. At a minimum, we will benefit from regularly taking a long walk or pausing to sit quietly and reflect on our life. Ideally, we will find a meditation practice that we can engage in daily.

Taking time for ourselves is essential to maintaining a connection with our higher self. It is in these precious moments that we either solidify our current path or find spiritual guidance and reconnect with our intended purpose. In this way, we leave our unique footprint on this human journey.

September 11

Happiness and Peace

Happiness and peace arise not from the pursuit of external goals or the entanglements of worry, expectation, and ambition, but through detachment from these distractions. True happiness and peace lies beyond the mind's fleeting concept of joy—in the quiet stillness that remains when the mind lets go.

Empathic Happiness and Peace can be found by opening our hearts to ALL fellow sentient travelers, free from all forms of judgment or jealousy.

Willful Happiness and Peace arise at our birth into this impermanent human existence and are experienced when we align our will with the Will of our Higher Power.

Humble Happiness and Peace cannot be experienced while attached to our economic condition, social status, or family roles.

A true sense of Happiness and Peace cannot be experienced without accepting suffering as an integral part of our human journey.

Pure Happiness and peace are experienced in moments of conscious contact with God as we understand Him.

September 12

Mindful Thinking

My life situations led to disillusionment, and I wrongly blamed those around me for my poor circumstances. Having recovered from a malady of the spirit, I began to exercise prudence of thought and word, and with a compassionate heart I escaped from the selfish practice of judging others.

Inner peace is disturbed by harmful or cynical thinking; therefore, we must avoid it. With persistent pessimism, we can relapse into old reactions or behaviors.

External conditions improve as our relationships with others and with the world stabilize. Through the daily development of a kind heart and mindful thinking, we're freed from malicious thoughts and come to naturally practice selfless compassion toward others.

September 13

Spiritual Connection to Others

Mind-altering substances, compulsive behaviors, delusional thoughts and emotions separate us from our true selves and from others. As part of our recovery, we shed dysfunctional habits, accept ourselves completely, and rebuild our connections with others.

As we become kinder to ourselves, stop practicing unwarranted self-criticism, cut out unrealistic expectations, and extinguish delusional thinking, we will begin to seek Spiritual Connection with others. This differs from typical social interaction in that Spiritual Connection is a deepened empathic bond. We transmit love, acceptance, and understanding through our undivided presence for those with whom we interact. We celebrate their joy and mourn their sorrow as our own.

Getting in sync with our Higher Self and with others will widen the gap between who we were and who we have become; from self-centeredness to selflessness, from emptiness to wholeness, from being apart to becoming part of.

September 14

Spiritual Guidance

Some claim that God came into their lives, this implies they lived without God for a period of time. Perhaps we assume that those not devoted to God live without His power, goodness, or spiritual direction.

Some report having had a spiritual experience, a white light moment. My experience, and the most common for all of us, is that of a growing closeness to a Higher Power through our thoughtful intention.

The Spirit of Love is within us from our first breath and remains with us until our parting. Even those who do not seek, who do not believe, or who even scoff at the idea of a power greater than themselves, cannot avoid Spiritual Guidance.

If the universe was to be without Spiritual Guidance, how would the sun know when to rise, the winds when to blow, or the flowers when to bloom? Without Spiritual Guidance, how would we know of love and compassion?

September 15

Reveal Your Hidden Picasso

Each of us is an artist who contributes to the canvas of life.

For a time, I felt unworthy and lacking in talent. I withdrew my participation from this human artistic endeavor. The conviction of unworthiness is a foolish judgment.

Our birth renders us artists with unlimited potential. Each with our own unique individual flair. No one brushstroke is more brilliant than another, no one color can claim primary importance. To withdraw our participation is to deprive the world of our given spiritual talent, our hidden Picasso. The beauty of our individual style lies in its variety. How dull a painting would be if it were of a single solid color. How uneventful a life that lacks spontaneity.

Step out of your protected predictable zone and join this abstract spiritual voyage. Let yourself immerse in all the colors of the rainbow and then throw them onto our common canvas, Reveal Your Hidden Picasso.

Without your participation, our life painting will lack your unique perspective, your loving contribution, and the masterpiece that is our journey cannot be considered complete.

September 16

The Loving Touch

As I allow all the mixed feelings and emotions to travel through my mind and soul on this anniversary of my mother's passing, I reflect on her life, her journey, her happiness.

Did she live freely as the person she wanted to be? Did she make the life choices she wanted to make? Sadly, the answer to both is no. My mother lived the parental and cultural script she was given at birth, rigorously and without missing a line. Sadly, she never gained insight or awareness of her Divine Freedom.

What brought her the most joy was her home. She worked to make sure it was always spotless, nothing out of place. On the outside, everything was always perfect. Inside there was a fluctuation of ups and downs, happiness and sadness. I pray that today she is at peace in a world without judgment.

I wonder if my mother ever knew how much I loved her. I rebelled against the script. I would give anything for one last conversation, one last hug, one last "I love you." I miss the soft, loving touch of my mother's hand today and every day.

September 17

Acceptance of The Truth

To think that I watched my life go up in flames before my eyes, and because of lack of inspiration, I let the fire burn. It was only at the very last gasp that I found the courage to reach out for help. This insanity has a name. It is called delusion. A dis-ease of a mind poisoned by years of consuming The Lie.

A lie that began as a comforting solution to my unhappy relationship with myself, others, and the world. In the end, it became my greatest enemy. It became clear that I was living against my values because I had abandoned realistic ideals and surrendered my will to The Lie. During these years I experienced moments of clarity, but the few were quickly extinguished.

My acceptance of The Truth came in a moment of Divine Intervention. It was not a conscious choice. I was led to The Truth. I unknowingly entered into a relationship with a Higher Power. The Truth promised and delivered a way to live free of delusion and in accordance with my values. It is in living The Truth that I find the solution to a happy relationship with myself, others, and the world.

September 18

The Lie

In times of irreconcilable conflict with self, others, and the world, we become susceptible to The Lie. Its disguises are numerous: food, gambling, drugs, alcohol, tobacco, shopping, work, money, sex, depression, and other methods used to numb painful emotions. It's like a game of whack-a-mole, get rid of one, and another pops up.

Even years into my recovery, I'm still disturbed by how many people are affected by The Lie. I share my story with some. They connect with The Lie and are baffled by how The Truth could be a solution to what destroyed their lives. I give much credit to the few who've risked such a change, many of whom come to experience long-lasting sobriety.

Regrettably, our human minds have difficulty accepting a spiritual solution to our troubles. I pray that those who are still under the spell of The Lie may experience their gift of desperation and encounter the grace to embrace and live The Truth.

September 19

Spiritual Treasure

The unhealthy competitiveness of the material world darkens our spirit. To be a "winner," one must step over a "loser." Being beaten for a parking space or losing millions of dollars in a deal gone bad has the same meaning to the spiritually unfit.

The game of ego-feeding deception ensnares the players. They choose a hostile, often cruel way of life. They believe it is a matter of survival. The players are so committed to this material, self-serving game that they fail to unlock their Spiritual Treasure.

We will benefit from moving away from rigid concepts of winners and losers, right and wrong, black and white. Living in moral ambiguity allows for more flexibility, reality, and compassion. We will also find gratitude for the offerings that life has gifted us.

Players are prisoners of resentment, jealousy, frustration, and fear of the unknown. Living with humble ambition opens the spiritual treasure that offers a life of contentment, trust, satisfaction, and faith.

September 20

Validation

Why run regularly, if I am not going to win any races, set any world records, or receive any awards? Why bother to write if few will read my words? Why reach out to someone if they won't reach out to me?

How delirious to think this way. Doing things for the purpose of approval is evidence of continued self-centeredness. Even if I received the recognition I sought, it would be short-lived because vanity is not easily satisfied.

The purpose of running, writing, or reaching out to others should be to bring joy. Caring for my body by running, my mind by writing, and my compassion for others by connecting with them is a choice for physical, mental, and spiritual well-being.

I spent a part of my life seeking validation and approval. While it is gratifying to have my efforts praised by others, it rarely matches the reward of inner comfort. Today I will run, write, and contact someone simply because it will bring joy.

September 21

Restraint of Thought

Thought is the mastermind behind all emotions, feelings and actions.

We're encouraged to practice restraint of pen and tongue and to choose carefully the words we write or speak, so that we communicate with sensitivity and respect rather than insult. Once unleashed, the spoken or written word cannot be taken back. Restraint of pen and tongue protects others from hurt and us from ridicule for regrettable actions.

But what about thoughts? Surely, we are free to think as we please, others cannot read our minds, and no harm can be done? While our thoughts may not have a direct impact on others, our spirit's light fades when we involve ourselves in character assassination. Nothing can harm our spirit like prejudice, judgment, jealousy, or anger.

Neutral thoughts do not exist. Thoughts feed our power of intention. Although we cannot control incoming thoughts, we have the ability to feed or starve them. By practicing humble, compassionate thinking, we curb our biases, praise our peers, and brighten the light of our spirit.

September 22

Forgiving Betrayal

There have been people in my life who have caused me great pain. Feelings of anger, resentment, and revenge accompanied the betrayal. These dark emotions bring temporary relief to the wounded soul. But they are monsters with an insatiable thirst. We would drain all the oceans of the world to quench their thirst.

Forgiveness allowed me to resume this complicated but morally unavoidable relationship. I could not allow stubbornness to darken my spirit. Forgiveness did not completely erase the hurt, nor did it erase all resentment. I've had to let the generosity of time to heal.

Forgiveness is a process by which prayer leads to spiritual guidance and dispels destructive thoughts that would otherwise consume my inner peace. The Light of Spirit has replaced resentment, hatred, and revenge with gratitude, love, and compassion.

To forgive is to make a conscious decision to let go of what has hurt us so we are free to love again.

September 23

Stick With the Winners

There are people in our lives whose spiritual aura stays with us forever. Anyone who takes part in our human excursion can be our master. In life's classroom, everyone is qualified to teach.

Once we are on the spiritual path, we attract people into our lives who inspire a better version of ourselves. Our Spiritual Guide has sent these individuals to deliver a teaching. We should seek to learn the nature of their spiritual aura and the practice they used to achieve it. In this way, we, too, become conduits of the Divine Power for good in the world.

The "winners" are mixed among us. They are those who live spiritual ideals. Their aura encapsulates their being, but it is only recognized by those who sincerely seek the Spiritual Way.

May we remain teachable in seeking, sensing, and Sticking With The Winners.

September 24

The Human Condition

Throughout history, humans have used their human traits and instincts to maintain mental, emotional, and physical stability.

Our species has developed a grave Human Condition. Modernization, and overpopulation have led to amplified forms of greed, jealousy, and resentment. Our human traits have adapted through enhanced self-centeredness and exclusion, making for catastrophic mayhem in our society.

There is a spiritual solution to our malady. Spiritual awareness, unlike instinct's temporal and spatial constraints, arises from communion with the Universe's Guiding Spirit, prioritizing His Will over our own. A selfless solution to that which overwhelms our human experience lies in our commitment to opening our hearts and minds to His grace.

September 25

A Loose Garment

Imagine a life where you'd wear a tuxedo or ball gown daily. We would experience unrelenting stress as we tried to avoid any situation that might tarnish our garment. Our attire would give us a false sense of self-importance. The smell of arrogance would precede us, causing instant misjudgment.

We can choose to shed our affluent disguise and put on our old favorite sweatshirt—the one with a few noticeable stains on the body and a moth hole in the sleeve—the one we snuggle into on the couch while enjoying a silly movie and a bowl of ice cream. While a drop of fudge on our outfit can be fixed with a quick wash, it would be a major disaster if it happened to our fancy tuxedo or gown.

Each day, we can choose to conform to the social norms that determine our fictitious status by wearing the ball gown or the fancy tuxedo, or we can choose to live an authentic life outside the reasonable judgment of others by wearing life like A Loose Garment.

September 26

Human Nature is Love

Our nature is love. All that exists in our soul is pure.

When I feel overwhelmed, I ought not question the emotion or try to ignore its effects. I should recognize its external origin and block it from interfering with my well-being. I should also not allow periods of euphoria to deceive me by permitting a sense of superiority or arrogance.

I try to stay balanced in my emotions throughout the day, which is best accomplished by habitually taking inventory of the purity of my intentions and allowing my inner spirit, not the outside world, to guide me.

I am grateful for the teachings that have brought me the simplicity of living one day at a time, guided by the spirit of my loving nature.

Only that for which I allow has power over me!

September 27

Alter Reality

A piece of chocolate soothes a moment of loneliness. A cup of coffee sparks motivation. A cigarette takes the edge off. Alcohol eases anxiety, serving as a deceptive social lubricant. And drugs—drugs wipe us clean of all emotion. Few are able to medicate using these methods for any length of time without suffering consequences. For the rest, whether due to genetic predisposition or spiritual deficit, they experience uncontrollable escalation and dysfunction.

A series of events carved a void in our souls, leaving space for destructive, fallible solutions from the outside world. Once mind-altering substances and behaviors are removed, we are once again left with a gaping void. Awareness and human power are not enough. Divine intervention is necessary to remove these compulsions, as they are beyond human control.

The solution to our emptiness lies in tapping into our infinite inner spiritual wealth. Knowledge and practice of fundamental Truths will help us recover from our obsessions and reject any desire to Alter Reality.

September 28

The Lake House

My mind is so restless that it causes internal, awkward emotional reactions to personalities and situations.

The most peace I experienced was at the Lake House. Nestled in the woods, sheltered by large oak trees, I spent many weekends there with my dogs in welcome solitude. The Lake House provided a spiritual refuge.

I realize now that discomfort has been with me all my life. I've tried to escape it in many ways. Outside of a very small circle of close relationships, there is an underlying doubt and discomfort in my interactions with others. What comes so naturally to some, I find challenging for myself.

Each day brings growth in my relationship with the God of my understanding. In His presence I feel completely accepted and free from judgment. Maybe my social expectations are unreasonable—perhaps I've simply never grown up.

September 29

The Crutch of Insanity

Awareness is present in our subconscious, for we have always known the cause of our suffering. Acceptance is allowing the awareness to surface and finding the courage to look it in the eye. The most challenging part of the healing process is letting go of our pride.

Unwilling to commit to this endeavor, and lacking immediate relief, we become discouraged and return to what we know. The mind chooses the path of inaction. Often, it will take increased suffering to surrender and accept guidance. Stubbornness is The Crutch of Insanity.

The path to healing lies in transcending what is ultimately a mental delusion—for if we followed true logic, we would take the steps necessary to heal. And yet, we often resist. We struggle to engage the spirit. Some remain unaware of its presence, while others grow bitter toward it. But healing requires a spiritual solution from within. It calls us to awaken, to reconnect with the Higher Self—our inner beacon of light and Truth.

Absent the Spirit's guidance, we're left to follow a mind lost in delusion.

September 30

Speaking From the Pure Heart

There are those who cannot express their thoughts or feelings and those who lack the ability to practice verbal restraint. A healthy balance is found in Speaking From the Pure Heart—a place of intentional love. It is this balance that I seek.

My tongue often malfunctions! Sometimes, words leave my mouth before my mind has a chance to filter them. When I say one thing but feel another, it's a sign the ego is overriding the spirit. I grow by practicing humility, even when it's clear someone is speaking in error or is led by their ego. There are three questions I could ask myself before expressing my opinion on any situation:

Does it need to be said? Comments, observations, or opinions do not always need to be expressed. Most of the time, what is left unsaid carries more weight than unnecessary self-serving words.

Does it need to be said now? It would serve me well to have a pause button to automatically mute my comments so that I can rethink the importance of what I am about to say and how I am about to say it. Time often reframes my original thought.

Does it need to be said by me? Although it is important for me to express my feelings or thoughts in certain situations, just as often, a situation will resolve itself best without my interference.

I examine where my words come from. The path or essence of the thought will shape its content or intent. Words spoken from hurt are unkind and easily forgotten. Words Spoken From the Pure Heart come from a place of love and have a lasting effect.

October 1

Healing the Pain

Throughout our lives we accumulate disappointments and hurts. Some individuals find that mind-altering substances provide a solution, others engage in compulsive behaviors to distract the pain, and still others live a life unaware of their emptiness.

Failed methods brought us peace for a time. Eventually, we became dependent on them for our emotional survival, and they became our masters, doubling our misery and stripping us of all dignity. We were at a loss, for no sincere promise or determined willpower allowed us to escape their grasp.

For a fortunate few, there comes a moment of clarity—a brief window of time when, spurred by suffering, we find unexpected strength. In that moment, we realize we cannot recover alone, and that no human power can truly heal our pain. We begin to accept the guidance of a power greater than ourselves—one that can fill our void and lead us back to wholeness.

The miracle of clarity we experience may be a once-in-a-lifetime experience. Once we have found a solution for healing the pain, we should cherish it as if it were our last breath of air. Like a frightened child clinging to its mother's hand, we will cling to the hand of our Higher Power. And in doing so, we will not be lost again.

October 2

The Hereafter

I am not afraid of "death" because I do not see it as an end.

For my message will live on.

Where my spirit goes does not concern me.

The love I leave behind will live on.

How I am seen afterward cannot affect my sense of purpose.

For what I have done will live on.

I'm not going to dwell on the struggles I've had.

For my overcoming will live on.

What remains undone does not define me.

For my achievements will live on.

I acknowledge and embrace both the light and the darkness within my life.

Both suffering and joy have prepared me for what's to come.

I have faith that I will experience forgiveness and peace in The Hereafter.

October 3

Spiritual Kindergarten

Before my involvement in a Twelve Step program, I had little understanding of spirituality. My early exposure to organized religion instilled more doubt than faith in a Higher Power.

The Twelve Steps became my spiritual kindergarten. It was there I learned the most basic concepts, beginning with the simple acceptance that I was not "God"; the world did not have to bow to my selfish wishes, desires, or commands. I was to become a worker among workers.

With this simple understanding, my spiritual journey began. I had lived recklessly, with little sense of responsibility or reverence—for others or for myself. If I hadn't been introduced to Spiritual Kindergarten, the Twelve Steps would never have become part of my daily life. I would have missed the gift of living by spiritual principles.

October 4

Becoming Ordinary

There was a void within me. I was invisible and wanted to be noticed, to feel that I mattered. My approach turned into an illusory quest for attention. I sought center stage, but there was never a big enough starring role.

While on this path, I lived in disappointment, always incomplete. I became bitter, envious, and insecure. Guided by the ego, I chased a shallow, unrealistic image. The unquenchable thirst for self-importance gave way to a desperation that bordered on insanity.

Every instance of attention proved temporary, succeeded by a more profound emptiness. To undo the damage of this lifestyle, one must first become aware of their inner daemons and then engage in spiritual healing.

Through the healing process, I acknowledged deficits in my upbringing that contributed to my dysfunction. This awareness allowed for an ongoing process of self-forgiveness and self-love.

The forces of ego are still at work, but today, they meet fierce resistance from awakened humility. Where emptiness once lived, there is now a quiet mind and the gentle grace of Becoming Ordinary.

October 5

Avoiding Selfishness

Selfishness can't be avoided—unless we choose to live guided by Divine Principles. For only by recognizing our place and purpose as one among many can we begin to let go of self-centeredness.

In these times, when the human race is beset with the tragedy of wars and fears of global extinction, we have used material accumulation as a source of distraction and comfort. When we detach from the anxiety caused by material concerns and become grateful for spiritual offerings, we no longer covet what is excessive.

Spiritual guidance will not eliminate turbulence from sentient life. Still, in striving to live according to the Divine Principles, our selfishness gives way to selflessness and we encounter a most priceless jewel: finding comfort and inner peace amid disorder and chaos.

October 6

Living Our Best Life

Happiness takes many forms. What delights one person may not appeal to another. Some find joy in travel, fine dining, and sharing their adventures in ways that highlight their prosperity. They want the world to see that they're living and loving their best lives. I feel joy for them—alongside a flicker of momentary jealousy at their vibrant experiences.

There are those less fortunate who will probably never experience such good fortune, but that does not mean they lack the blessings of life. We can live our best lives on a luxury cruise or in an old canoe floating down a lazy river. A weekend at a fancy hotel or in a pop-up tent in a sleepy forest. Dining on nouvelle cuisine at a popular bistro or enjoying a quaint dinner at home with friends.

Let's refrain from judging and envying how others live. Loving and living our best life is a state of mind. Wealthy is he who fills his heart with gratitude for his lot and prays that all others may share in the varied riches of life.

October 7

Unmanageability

People struggling with addiction, both substance and behavioral, eventually recognize their lives are unmanageable. Loss of job, family, or reputation are high bottoms. Loss of shelter, food, and health are just around the corner. These make it clear that life has become ungovernable.

As quality of life deteriorates and the returns from their drug of choice diminish, thoughts of ending the nightmare begin to surface. It becomes a matter of choosing life over death. That this is a ponderable choice speaks to the insanity of the insidiousness of addiction. But so it is!

For many of us, only an act of Providence saved our lives from the abyss. Having been restored to sanity, we share our grief and our hope so that others may find the same grace of redemption.

October 8

Detachment

We cannot achieve the ideal of being or living our authentic selves as long as people, expectations, or situations hold us back.

We come to know our true selves only as we learn to detach from the good opinion of others and from our own self-judgment. Detachment is the key that frees us from blindly seeking the approval of harsh, unforgiving, relentless human expectations.

Detachment may be an ideal, but it's a gentle practice worth leaning into—and one we can continue striving for, little by little. Detachment doesn't make me a desert island, it simply defines the boundaries of my spiritual well-being. When I am detached, I become a willing participant with healthy boundaries and at no time am I consumed by people, expectations, or situations. Although chaos may be all around me, I do not allow it to cross my personal or spiritual boundaries.

The Great Spirit, in His infinite wisdom, power, and love, is the sole source of unconditional understanding and acceptance.

October 9

Correcting Character Flaws

After years of self-will running riot, during which I directed my efforts toward controlling everything in my sphere, I could not realistically expect spiritual order to be restored without the resurrection of moral values.

My emotions and decisions were shaped by how others viewed me. When I experienced conflict, I focused on the other's shortcomings. Self-centered conceit obscured my wrong in any situation.

I began correcting my character flaws by honest self-appraisal and then by taking ownership of my thoughts and actions. Through consistent self-reflection, I learned how my limitations muddied my relationship with myself and others.

Only after I became aware of my shortcomings, did the work of moral recovery begin. Through sincere effort, I became genuinely willing to make amends for wrongs done to my fellows.

In prayer, I ask to be freed from self-centeredness. In meditation, I ask that Higher Will be revealed and that spiritual order be restored.

October 10

United by Spirit

From a very early age, I felt different from others. Going to boarding school with individuals from a different social class was challenging. Moving to a new country with a foreign language was challenging. I dressed differently. I thought differently. My experiences and cultural norms were different. I felt like a puzzle piece that couldn't find its place, no matter how hard I tried to fit in. I learned to mimic their ways, even the dysfunction, but inside, I felt estranged.

This was to manifest in my life through many years of addiction.

Desperation led me to join a fellowship made up of outsiders. A sense of estrangement from the world unites the group's members. By sharing our experiences, we discover a common thread that bonds us. Our inner loneliness gave way to kinship. Often, only someone who has walked in the same tight-fitting shoes can understand our deep sorrow, disillusionment, and peril.

We are all not without uniqueness, yet we are all of equal value in the eyes of the Great Friend, and together, we are united in the Spirit.

October 11

Honesty and Courage

We choose to practice Honesty and Courage in our daily lives by showing up, speaking our Truth, and living our Truth.

Honesty and Courage with ourselves involve challenging patterns of behavior that have become ingrained in us—patterns that we've allowed to define us but that we no longer find acceptable. Honesty with self involves acknowledging our wrongs, recognizing our good, and having the Courage to follow a new path.

Honesty and Courage are accessible to us through acceptance of spiritual guidance. When we follow direction, we need not worry about our choices; rightness or wrongness, for the Spirit's righteousness guides us.

October 12

Accept and Adapt

There is a quiet wisdom in nature that reminds us how to live with grace. Animals are guided by pure spirit without complication, intention without ego.

We humans, too, possess this spiritual intuition, yet it often lies buried beneath the clutter of our mental and emotional struggles. These challenges, often delusional in nature, dominate our human condition and cloud our clarity.

What our pets model so naturally is a kind of graceful surrender. No matter what changes around them, they simply Accept and Adapt. In moments of inner turmoil, this is the wisest path I can follow.

The difference between my pets and me is that I often resist; I fight, moan, or procrastinate before I am pushed to finally Accept and Adapt to life's inevitable changes.

To move through life's inevitable challenges with greater peace, I must take a lesson from them: return to simplicity, let go of resistance, and, with quiet strength, Accept and Adapt.

October 13

Need For Approval

A major driving force in my life was the need for my parent's approval. I was successful until I reached my teenage years when we drifted apart ideologically. My mad curiosity and instinct for independence consumed me. Preoccupied with realizing their dream, my parents lovingly wrote the script for my predetermined role.

Subconsciously, I rebelled. I wanted the freedom to choose my destiny. A tug- of-war ensued, and neither of us sought a resolution. Despite our happy moments, resentment slowly deepened until it eroded into mistrust.

My refusal to accept, respect, or obey dismayed them. I felt betrayed, unheard and dismissed. This became fertile ground for years of my self-destruction which caused us both much pain. Our stubborn inability to communicate or compromise, combined with the short-sightedness of our selfish desires, robbed us of serenity and connection.

Through my spiritual awakening, I escaped the grip of addiction and the destructive need for approval or self-importance. I can now acknowledge, accept, respect, and forgive us for the love we lost and fondly cherish the love we shared.

October 14

Pure Thought - Pure Living

How am I to distinguish purity from impurity? It is not always clear.

Pure thought is selfless. It leads me to love and understanding. I can feel the warmth of purity in my heart and bathe in its radiance. It leads to pure living.

Impure thought is selfish. It leads me to judge others or to selfish indulgence. I feel uncomfortable, confused, anxious. It leads to impure living.

I welcome and embrace pure thoughts. I dance with them for they bring me joy.

I refuse access to impure thoughts. I question their validity and promptly dismiss them by giving them no importance.

Spirit Consciousness, a level of consciousness beyond human capacity, rightly judges the purity of thought.

When we connect with Spirit Consciousness and allow ourselves to be guided by its pure intention, we will identify and deny impure thought, embrace Pure Thought, and give rise to Pure Living.

October 15

Putting It Off

We postpone prayer for the first twenty years.

We know not of it.

For the next twenty years, we are too busy with life's challenges, for time is precious, and we have much to accomplish.

Prayer is of little use to our logic.

Over the following twenty years, lives take form, and routines develop.

We became comfortable living this way.

For the next twenty years, we enjoy the fruits of our labor, for our work is done.

Prayer is no longer necessary.

In the next twenty years, we will reach our earthly end.

This is the story of an empty life.

Our earthly existence will find deeper meaning if we engage in spiritual practice. We may wish we had not put off prayer, for it would help us better understand our spiritual purpose.

October 16

The Addict

Addiction is an ugly disease; it lies, steals, manipulates, intimidates, and angers all who are afflicted and all who come in contact with The Addict. It often arises to fill an inner void; as such, it is no more a choice than opening a damaged parachute at five thousand feet and hoping for a soft landing. We might see those struggling with addiction as a casualty of a damaged human spirit.

We help by creating the conditions for recovery by offering reality-based solutions. We throw them a rope in the hope that they will be willing to pull themselves toward the light. When help is refused, we can only watch and pray from afar, hoping the damaged parachute catches enough air to slow them down before impact.

We must never give up hope, for they too are of pure spirit. Our pain pales in comparison to the despair of trying to stay afloat while being dragged down by a disease so powerful that it defies a human solution. The path of recovery is rarely gentle; the individual must ultimately face the consequences and take responsibility for the harm caused—but this, too, is part of their healing process.

Do not fear their outward ugliness, but look upon them with compassion, for in their soul resides the Divine potential to restore their dignity.

October 17

Sprouting Flaws

My character flaws grew from an underlying fear that I was not good enough.

To admit that I might have made a mistake would confirm my inner doubts, so I lied, and when I was not believed, I became angry. With anger came resentment, with resentment came a sense of entitlement; this was self-centeredness. When I didn't get what I wanted, I felt betrayed, which led to self-pity.

Shame and guilt grew within me for violating the basic morals I had learned in my youth. My addiction justified my many wrongs.

With recovery came a willingness to change. Weakened pride gave way to humility. To maintain my temperament, I keep a watchful eye on the inevitable sprouting of what remains of my faults. Perfection of character is illusory. Improvement through humility is inevitable.

October 18

Reputation

Reputations are such that, for many, addicts remain forever tarnished. The stain of self-centered arrogance is not easily washed away. The time I have left on this earthly journey may not be enough to undo the whirlwind of chaos I once unleashed. There is always a cost—such is the nature of karma.

My selfish actions have caused many to withdraw from my life and yet there are so many others who have witnessed only my grace. Gone is the awkwardness of questioning my purpose. Regrets inspire my benevolence and spirit of service.

In sobriety, we write a new chapter. With our reputation still embedded in their minds, some will hold back from experiencing our awakened spirit. For them we pray.

Having overcome our bruised humility and now guided by the Spirit, we live on, spreading love and peace with those who walk with us on the road to a happy destiny.

October 19

Intended Purpose

We each develop a unique set of skills that matches our natural and spiritual abilities. We will instinctively know which path to choose. When we follow the intended path, we'll experience fulfillment in our purpose.

There are external factors that condition our choices and we may start out disoriented. In this case, our spiritual inner voice signals the need for change in perfect timing with the circumstances of our life. Should we heed the spiritual alert, we will accept guidance toward our intended purpose.

Resistance to spiritual guidance often results in inner conflict. Some live a lifetime of inner dissatisfaction or turmoil, unaware of its source.

By accepting and surrendering to what is truly meant for us the moment our spirit calls, we fulfill our purpose and soften the suffering of our human journey.

October 20

Hope

Prayer and meditation are experiences of communicating with and receiving guidance from the Divine Life Source. It is the way in which I have come to connect and continue to grow a deeper and more meaningful relationship with my inner self.

I live each day with the intention of creating a better tomorrow. To create positive energy by being the best imperfect being I can be. I am in an eternal search for the "who" I am meant to become. On the path to a place of peace where there is total acceptance of the past, present, and future.

No matter how challenging my life situation may be, I choose to seek the speck of light within the darkness—a light I truly believe to be Hope.

October 21

Spiritual Conditioning

Spiritual conditioning is the process by which we detach from the rigid programming instilled in us by societal, religious, and cultural norms and become free to express our individuality without judgment.

We condition the spirit by developing spiritual knowledge, and through spiritual growth, we become empowered to think what we think and speak what we think. It is a free-flowing, uninterrupted process that breaks through the myths of human programming. We live as we choose, without fear of judgment, but guided by spiritual principles.

We transform into a matter of being that transcends the nonsense of complying with complicated, convoluted norms and adheres to a meaningful existence guided by the Natural Order of the Universe.

October 22

The Wondrous Universe

When I look at the natural beauty of the universe—its endless oceans, majestic forests, a bee pollinating a flower, a deer leaping freely across a field— I ask myself,: "How? Who? What orchestrates this perfectly tuned natural symphony? To me, it's evidence of a Universal Intelligence—a Spiritual Maestro conducting all of life, and we, too, are instruments in that grand design.

When we detach from the burdens of our minds, from the tedious self-direction, and consciously connect with the universal flow, we experience natural peace. These moments arise from dedicated spiritual work. Sitting quietly for a few moments and connecting with the rhythm of our breath or taking in the wonders of a passing cloud brings us closer to Universal Intelligence.

It is in the process of deep spiritual effort and in our earnest desire to connect with the Wondrous Universe that we find liberation and joy.

October 23

Fully conditioned

We become fully conditioned to the material life. Be it family or financial, employment or friends, it is nearly impossible to escape society's demands. I become agitated and uneasy with life's traditional routines. Most, not by choice, survive through compliance, adapting to whatever each season demands.

I want to run from the world as it is.

To be free to roam without care and to never look back.

Perhaps this is common to us all.

It is unrealistic and I do well to stay within the limited boundaries of a world that I alone created. To escape the material view, I tune into my spirit's voice. From within come echoes of joy for that is the nature of a free spirit. My spirit is thankful for life but wonders about my impatience. It knows not of delusional expectation.

When experiencing frustration from the rigidness of the material view, I seek refuge and find peace within the limitless confines of my spirit.

October 24

Lord I Seek

Lord, I seek the end.

For I desire a new beginning.

In times of deep inner sadness, I reflect on how I came to be. I've identified the selfish choices I made along the way, as they lie at the heart of the emotional imbalance I once experienced.

It is wounding to look karma in the eye and feel a dagger of remorse. I alone cannot escape sorrow; in communion with the Eternal Heart, I find self-forgiveness. Prayer allows me liberation from the material form of my mind and to join the Unseen Spirit in a harmonious daily reprieve.

Lord, I thank thee for the love you provide, for it will carry me forward and without regret, for another day.

October 25

The Crutch

In times when we are unable to accept what we cannot change, nor have the courage to change what we can, our lives become unbalanced. A crutch becomes a resource for equilibrium, fertile ground for dis-ease of mind, body, and spirit to thrive.

When circumstances beyond our control arise, such as grief, injustice, or sorrow, our best recourse is to rely on the Spiritual Source to prevent substances, compulsive behaviors, self-pity, depression, or dishonesty from becoming our crutch.

In times of instability, I rely on my Higher Power as my crutch. I become willing to ask for acceptance of my circumstances, courage to change them, and wisdom to discern which option will bring about spiritual balance.

The Journey of Recovery

October 26, 2022

A Humble Servant

Service is the path that connects self-centeredness to selflessness.

As long as I can remember, awkwardness has accompanied me. Through natural experimentation with mind-altering substances and behaviors, I found relief from constant self-consciousness and my critical self-regard. It ultimately backfired, leaving me oscillating between crippling self-doubt and unwarranted arrogance, a pattern that repeated itself until my inevitable crash.

When I became aware of what I had become, I knew I had to change. I found the solution in a recovery program—living a life grounded in moral principles, nurtured by spiritual awareness, and connected to a Higher Power.

Reversing the process takes commitment, discipline, faith, and time. The key is to become a humble servant. Being of service to others has become the purpose of my journey. It begins with those closest to me and extends to developing understanding, empathy, and compassion for all beings.

It is impossible to accomplish this noble feat in one lifetime.

October 27

Chance The Unknown

We dared not risk the unknown.

We grew older and wiser like the great oak.

We gained awareness.

The day comes when we acknowledge the goals we have not yet achieved.

Let us waste no more time. Let the future begin now.

Principled living has brought self-reverence, and with it we must summon the courage to leave the safety of the known and use the last sands of time to realize what has been left undone.

If you can imagine it, then it is possible.

If it has a name, then it exists.

Dare to pursue the quest that lies before you in the unknown.

October 28

People Pleasing

People Pleasing came about when I formed the belief that if I was genuine, I would fall short of expectations.

As a child, I used this form of manipulation by exaggerating my accomplishments to please my parents. My insecurity as an adult drove me to people-please, seeking validation to hide my shortcomings.

People pleasing succeeds only with those as shallow as the perpetrator; others see through the charade as phony, fake, or fraudulent. Trying to please everyone won't earn you genuine respect.

It's taken years and much soul searching to come out from behind the curtain and show my true self. The one that is confident, honest, genuine, and no longer fears the judgment of others. Today I strive to allow the full exposure of my imperfect humanity, for I accept that perfection exists only in the Kingdom of the High Spirit.

October 29

Optimism – Pessimism

I have a choice of how to interpret life situations. I can look at them with self-pity, "why does everything happen to me?" or "what is wrong with me?" Being a victim offers a peculiar sense of fulfillment. When I am a victim, I don't have to take responsibility for my actions or my pessimism. Though the victim role brings negative emotions, I grew so used to it that it became irrationally comfortable.

Inevitably, there will be another obstacle to overcome, another challenge to face, or another goal to achieve. Optimism requires action. If a wall gets in my way, instead of throwing up my arms and surrendering, today I find a way around it.

Pessimism breathes negativity and darkness into my spirit. Optimism breathes hope, confidence, and faith. I have a choice in how I decode a life event. I can choose to whine about the "why" of the circumstance, or I can be gracious in the "what" of the lesson I am about to learn. At various points in our lives, we're all faced with this choice.

October 30

Debilitating Torment

To resolve situations or change my life, I must act and be willing to work. Procrastination leads to self-inflicted suffering and inactivity until the repercussions become clear. What is stopping me from doing what I need to do? From saying what I have to say? I lack willingness. I lack the belief that the action I am about to take will result in "my" intended outcome.

Willingness involves faith. I must trust and accept that the action I take may not result in the way I wish, but in the way it should. This is the way of a Spiritual Universe. We do not wish for a rainy day, but if the rain does not come, our garden will wither. We seem to remain focused on single-minded, selfish desires, while the Universe provides us with what we need.

The need for an assured result is a paralyzing agent, and so I take the action deemed necessary. I say what needs to be said or I do what needs to be done. I then place the result in the hands of the One Wiser than I, the Power that will do for me what I cannot do for myself.

By letting go of outcomes, growing my willingness and my faith, I will cease to procrastinate and become free from Debilitating Torment.

October 31

Burnout

Burnout occurs when the mind is overloaded beyond its human limitations. We become susceptible to this phenomenon when we do not allow life to flow freely. Instead, we cling to every emotion, every circumstance, intent on changing the outcome of the inevitable.

The realm of spirit knows not of burnout; controlling the outcome is recognized as a futile effort. We are not without influence, for we are the vehicle, but we are best guided on this human journey by a loving spiritual guide who knows of our ignorance and doubt, but also of our untapped potential. It will challenge us, but never give us more than we can handle, for Spirit also knows our human limitations.

To avoid burnout of the mind, we let go of control, doubt, and outcome and allow for the guidance of a Loving Spirit.

November 1

The Teacher

I did not know how to be a supportive partner. I was blind to the intimate needs of another. I was first concerned about the impact on me and then about the impact it'd have on others. This became an instinctive process, conditioned and reinforced by past experiences. Ultimately, it led to dysfunctional relationships doomed by my wrongs.

A new connection brought new hope for a lasting romantic partnership. This time, I would do things differently because I'd grown tired of avoiding the obvious—all past relationships had one thing in common: me. I had to change. Perhaps I would become more attentive to this new teacher.

There have been challenging days in the classroom. I am learning sensitivity, selflessness, respect, empathy and humility. I struggled on my first tests, but my teacher was patient with my slow progress. She never gave up, even though there may have been times when she questioned my commitment. All I needed to master were the basics; there is no advanced study for practicing collaboration.

I still stumble when old instincts creep up, but I recover quickly. My past actions weigh heavily on me now that I fully understand the pain I've inflicted. I've grown from them into a caring, supportive partner. I have learned that there is no graduation, and I am committed to the ongoing lessons from my teacher.

November 2

Alone I Am Small

Alone, I was too small, too frail to carry the burdens of my life.

There were expectations I could not meet, challenges I was too weak to face, and doubts and worries that darkened my hopes and dreams. Except for a few brief periods of light, I had lived this way for most of my life.

Then, one bright summer morning, in a moment of quiet desperation, I unexpectedly made a seemingly insignificant decision that would change the course of my life. Suddenly, I felt a connection to a Divine Power, one that I now understand has always existed but only recently awakened my consciousness.

Decades later, I'm strong enough to carry the full load of my life. Expectations, challenges, difficulties, and worries have not disappeared, for they define my humanity. The strength to stand tall and meet each of them is provided by my spiritual communion with The Limitless Divine Power. All I am asked in return is to surrender my misguided self-will to His spiritual vision.

Through the Spirit's potential, I discovered the Kingdom, Power and the Glory to lead a fulfilling and meaningful life.

November 3

The Magic Wand

Although our first thoughts are unpredictable and often precarious, they can be tamed. Like a magic wand, well-considered second thoughts can magically change negative situations into positive ones—turning dust to gold.

While we should give meaning to every thought, we must nurture and feed the positive ones and starve the negative ones. A tiny window of time passes between the birth of a thought and its emotional impact. In that space of time, through conscious reflection, we accept productive or positive thoughts, and bid farewell to the delusional.

Our Higher Self, the watcher and guide of our journey, uses its magic wand to understand our impractical, seemingly wasteful thoughts, transforming them into introspective insights into the workings of our minds.

We do well to examine our most destructive thoughts, for they contain clues to patterns and behaviors that we may wish to eliminate in order to experience lasting peace.

November 4

Decision-Making

We are not alone and need not decide alone.

Seeking guidance is always beneficial, as we may overlook something. We can seek guidance from a mentor or other individuals who know us well and whom we have high regard. This input is like a safety valve, a second look at our reasoning.

Having received human guidance, we will continue the process by entering into communion with our Spiritual Guide and seeking spiritual guidance. During this process we quietly listen for the whisper from within. When connected to our Higher Self, we feel calm and become intuitive to higher will.

Having made our decision, we accept that it is now in the caring hands of our Higher Power. Believing this removes doubt and provides peaceful confidence that our decision will arrive at its spiritually intended port.

November 5

Let Go and Let God

Imagine standing at the door of an airplane, getting ready to plummet 10,000 feet to the ground. The butterflies in your stomach beating faster as the moment nears. Time to push off! Let Go and Let God. The initial free fall is terrifying, but there is little time to dwell on negativity.

From the moment we surrendered to this adventure, we had built-in faith that the parachute would open at our request. We pulled the cord, the parachute opened and we suddenly felt grateful and safe. We float effortlessly to our chosen landing site.

In life, we often procrastinate, prolonging the inevitable. We lose sleep tossing and turning, wrestling with what will be the "right" decision. If only we were quicker to Let Go and Let God instead of fighting for illusory control over an indeterminable outcome.

Procrastination is caused by fear of the outcome. I fear "failure." To overcome fear, I must let go of control. Letting go allows me to move on to my next challenge or venture. Procrastination is time wasted.

I remind myself that without fail, every time I have pulled the God cord, the spiritual shoot has opened, and I have landed safely at the place He intended, most often beyond my wildest imagination. When I Let Go and Let God, I put my faith into action.

November 6

Surrender

I had lost direction.

My life had become unmanageable.

I had unwittingly surrendered my ability to choose.

At times, I sensed that I had strayed from the right path and was not living in alignment with my true purpose. I believe that these instances were perpetuated by a watchful Guiding Spirit.

Reclaiming sovereignty over my life meant giving up what I had become and surrendering to a promised but unknown outcome. Living on the margins of insanity seemed unrealistic. How can we know what we cannot imagine? It is in desperation and blind faith that we initiate liberation from the pain of our mere existence.

Surrender means giving up our coercive will and partnering with recovered others in living a spiritual solution. Only through surrender do we shatter our resistance, regain the power of choice, and realize our purpose.

November 7

Purifying The Mind

Our real selves went into exile due to unacceptable shame, and we were left with our masked, pretend, delusional selves. To onlookers, we seemed utterly self-absorbed; however, we were actually struggling to survive via dysfunctional, destructive emotional masquerading.

As a result of our spiritual awakening, we've come to see ourselves as worthy—and we're willing to embark on the journey of self-actualization. In doing so, our true selves feel safe enough to emerge once again.

As we come to understand our troubled minds and practice newfound humility and honesty, we let go of our shame and embrace that which has shamed us.

The pure ocean water was inadvertently unpurified by salt from the land and ocean floor and so were our pure minds unpurified by delusional interpretations of life events.

Ocean water is purified through desalination, the mind is purified through the awakening of the spirit.

November 8

The Great Reality

Serenity arrives when we accept things as they are. Were we to believe otherwise, we would deny the Great Reality.

We can wage war against delusional forces and conspiracies created in our minds. In this way, we create suffering. Suffering imagines beyond the Great Reality—The Now. Although we experience emotional disturbances that seem real, they are often reactions to projected outcomes of situations yet to come.

To ease suffering, we diligently search within ourselves for the light of the Spirit. There, we find solace and guidance. Communion with Spirit banishes all suspicion, doubt, and projection from our minds. We become stronger than the circumstances of life.

Spiritual transformation changes the roaring storm of a thought ago into a soft, warm breeze embodied in the acceptance of the Great Reality.

November 9

Respect

We demanded respect from those around us. Perhaps we did not deserve such respect because our way was selfish and arrogant.

We considered ourselves kind-hearted, but closer examination revealed our kindness served our self-interest, and our giving expected something in return.

In recovery, the desire for a clean inventory replaces our concern for defending our misplaced honor. Our actions and thoughts demonstrate our adherence to fundamental moral values. Our self-respect takes precedence over the desire for the approval of others.

Demanding and expecting respect is for the delusional. One earns respect through selfless, inspired actions.

November 10

Show Up For Life

There are mornings when my delirious mind awakens before my spiritual inner self. By the time I am fully conscious, it has planned my day and often traveled far into the future. This triggers my fears and insecurities about the unknown and my ability to meet my obligations. Rarely is there any real validity to these delusions.

There have been mornings when I've pulled the covers over my head and let fear win. But to overcome fear, I plant my feet on the ground and Show Up For Life. I challenge delusional thoughts by grounding myself spiritually and returning to the present moment. Delusion resides in the future, in the now, it loses all its power.

Once present, I can show up for any of life's many challenges with the confidence that I am good enough and have the capacity to perform at the level that the Divine Power for Good in the World has intended for me.

I am only responsible for the effort, not the outcome!

November 11

The Spiritual Source

From the beginning, the human species has developed a belief in a power greater than itself. All civilizations, including the Aborigines, the Greeks, the Romans, the Incas, the great African tribes, the Buddhists, the Christians, the Jews, and the Muslims, have accepted the guidance of a great power that influenced the way they approached their lives, their destiny, and their afterlife.

We come to believe or not to believe, worship, fear, or to ignore this Omnipotent Power. Even non-believers, in times of great crisis, must wonder, if only for a moment, if there might be Divine intervention.

I choose to enrich my relationship with the Spiritual Source daily. In doing so, I feel more connected to the planet, my inner being, and all the individuals I encounter on this journey.

We can choose to live under the influence of our delusional mind or accept the guidance of our Inner Survival Instinct.

November 12

At the Speed of God

God is just another word for Universal Intelligence or Divine Order. Replace any image of God that does not serve you or blocks your mind from being open to infinite possibility and create your own image of Universal Intelligence.

Find a place in nature untouched by human hands—whether it's a majestic mountain, the vastness of the ocean or a glorious sunset. Let yourself merge with it. Let it move through you. We are not separate from these wonders; we are part of them. We are all part of Infinite Possibility.

The world has focused on an alternate reality created by our minds. Go to any major city and marvel at what the human mind has constructed: skyscrapers with their necks in the clouds, airplanes flying overhead, genius engineering that went into building the subway system under your feet. It's amazing, but not pure, not natural. We don't connect to it the way we connect to nature.

We can follow our minds—which are like boisterous, noisy, and turbulent cities—or we can follow Universal Intelligence, found in nature's quiet simplicity. The mind, like the city, moves at an unusually fast pace. Nature moves at the speed of God.

November 13

Be!

Living in faith offers no assurance that everything will work out the way we would have it, but it does guarantee that the outcome will be as it should be. There is a calm that follows every storm. I am neither the storm nor the calm. I am a spiritual being witnessing both. As such, I have three choices.

Be in the storm.

Be in the calm.

Be!

November 14

Offer No Resistance

Trees bend, dance, and sway with the wind, offering no resistance.

Fish swim with the current and offer no resistance.

Man is resistant to the obvious.

We're called to accept what we cannot change and to find the strength to change what we can. But too often, we distort the Truth—reshaping logic to serve our desires. Man lives not by Truth but by the impressions his mind allows.

We are unable to undo our past exposures or the effects of years of rigid social conditioning. But we can distance ourselves by taking refuge in the temple of our soul—a place of neutrality of thought that offers rest to a weary mind. Personal quiet time each day allows for perspective, realization of the brevity of our human journey, and gratitude for all that surrounds us.

Surrender to change like leaves in an autumn wind; bend, dance, and flow with the universe's Higher Consciousness.

November 15

The Sixth Sense

The five human senses are the communication channels between our mind and the material world. But there is also a sixth sense—one we must seek to experience a more profound Truth. The sixth sense is the channel of communication between our hearts and GOD.

The sixth sense reveals itself only when we shift from the material to the spiritual realm. We often access it in times of distress, but we tend to ignore it otherwise. It rests just beneath the surface of conscious thought, waiting for our attention. Yet, few of us take the time to truly connect with it. The mind naturally clings to what it can see, hear, smell, taste, or touch—what it can validate with the five senses.

The sixth sense is that of Good Orderly Direction. When I sense a rainbow on the horizon, I see GOD. When I hear the chirping of a robin in the early morning, I hear GOD. When the scent of spring flowers reaches me, I smell GOD. When I drink from a mountain stream, I taste GOD. And when I feel the soft skin of my mother's hand, I touch GOD.

As these thoughts flow from my heart to this page, I am being guided by GOD!

November 16

Daunting Temptation

Taking pictures is a way to capture precious memories. Too often, I have placed more importance on the photograph than on being present for the memorable moment.

This took on a new perspective when social media infiltrated my life. I fell into the trap of boosting my self-esteem by distorting my reality to appear sophisticated, interesting, or adventurous. The thrill of bragging outweighed the gratitude for my experiences.

My flaunting glorified the outer self while denying inner self-doubt. I never shared my dark emotions, fears, challenges, or insecurities. No amount of complementary "comments" or "likes" can build lasting self-worth.

The pervasiveness of social media is here to stay. It has become part of world culture. I do not want to diminish its importance. As with any other of life's frills, it is I who must be responsible and balanced. I find comfort in having become aware of my exhibitionism and having curbed my swagger for yet another of life's ego-centric Daunting Temptations.

November 17

The Human Puzzle

We often judge our worth by comparing ourselves to others. In reality, each of us is just a small piece of a large human puzzle, and each of us has been given equal value.

When we put together a puzzle, we interlock all the knobs and holes. Each piece fits seamlessly into the other, and each finds its rightful place. The next piece is always the most important, and each gets a turn at being the most significant. Only when each piece has found its place is the big picture fully revealed.

So it is in life. The Master Craftsman of the Universe has a purpose for each of us; if one were missing, the Universe would be out of balance and could not function to its perfection. Each of us has a purpose to contribute to human harmony.

Should we validate our contribution, we will understand our worth. Like the last piece of a puzzle, only after our last breath will our full works be revealed.

November 18

Sharing Our Challenges

As beginners in the recovery process, when we experience emotional turmoil, it is suggested that we reach out and share our struggles with another; this frees our troubles from darkness and isolation. Our delusions cower when exposed to the light.

However, there is a line that is crossed when our sharing becomes self-pity and we become helpless victims. We will have begun to empower our difficulties instead of finding solutions. In these times, we retreat to the quiet place in our heart, enter into communion with our Higher Power, and ask directly that we be relieved of our difficulty.

With consistent spiritual practice, we learn to distinguish well-intentioned sharing from self-destructive venting.

We discover when it's best to share our challenges with another and when it's time to let go, humbly placing them in the hands of our Higher Power.

November 19

Hitting Our Target

In the material world we are meant to figure things out, to come up with solutions. There are tasks that need just that, a solution, but our life is not a mathematical, mechanical or a logistical task. It's a journey, a spiritual experience.

In the realm of spirit, our purpose is to be of service to each other and to the universe. A life dedicated to figuring out a nonexistent equation is a life that has missed its target.

Like the flowing waters of a river that have great power to shape the landscape, let your life flow naturally, without resistance, to its intended destination, touching with love and service the many other beings who share the same journey.

When we have accomplished this task, we will have Hit Our Target.

November 20

Bridging the Gap

I face the challenge of reconciling outer turbulence with inner spiritual calm. True peace arises when I accept that earthly limitations often stand between me and my desired expectations.

Earthly desires offer only temporary comfort to my sentient mind. This mind, though a powerful instrument, is bound by earthly laws—limited by both time and space. Such desires rely on circumstances beyond our control, while spiritual longings are nonmaterial and transcendent, rooted in love and pure intention.

We can only bridge the gap between inner spiritual calm and outer turbulence through Spiritual Practice.

November 21

We Give It Away!

When addiction took hold of my life, I lived an alternative lifestyle. My priorities changed dramatically, and I distanced myself from moral principles. I emotionally isolated from family and friends. This is what addiction does—it demands separation and thrives on isolation, all while feeding us seductive, delusional reasoning.

When recovery arrived, I felt alone. Those who loved me deemed me untrustworthy—I had betrayed their trust—and I could no longer surround myself with my old cronies. This is a predicament of early sobriety.

My Twelve-Step group of spiritual nomads filled the social void. Through our shared experience—and survival—of a deadly disease, a deep understanding has formed. As we heal, we become not only valued members of the group but also more present and responsible in all affairs. The group becomes a bridge—one that leads us back to life.

Even after years in sobriety, we stay active and engaged in our group, knowing that continued participation is vital for sustaining our recovery. By sharing our experiences and survival, we help the lonely and lost newcomer find identification and hope.

We cannot keep it unless We Give It Away!

November 22

Inspire Change

We cannot control or willfully bring about change in others. We can, however, bring about change in ourselves. Having a spiritual experience changes everything about us. Our memories will be but a shadowy reminder of our past. Some pleasant, others hurtful. The combined experiences have brought us to this new and recovered version of ourselves.

We realize that the change we've experienced was made possible by following the example of those who modeled a spiritual path for us. While they did not change us, their influence played a vital role in our growth.

In the same way, our own lives—now rooted in spiritual grace—will Inspire Change in our families and friends. This shift won't come through willful control, but through the quiet power of living authentically.

November 23

Unbelief

On the journey of recovery, we conquer unbelief.

We are transformed from doubters to believers as we witness the transformation of the newcomer just days after his surrender, through the testimonies of miraculous spiritual rebirth shared by the old timers, and through our daily personal conquests over cravings, compulsions, and harmful behaviors.

Although our faith and trust in a power greater than ourselves has grown, we recognize the lingering doubt and unbelief. We see this as welcome motivation and reminder of the spiritual work yet to be done.

We do not become one with the Most High Spirit until we join him in the hereafter. However, we will feel His presence more deeply as we continue on the path of recovery and spiritual growth.

Of the realm of the spirit, we were resistant skeptics. As the gifts of sobriety slowly materialize, we become grateful believers.

November 24

Forgiveness

Although hurtful moments are not forgotten, forgiveness soothes the sorrow. Forgiving is not forgetting—it's finding resolve in situations that cannot be changed.

Too often, we view painful situations superficially or one-sidedly. It would serve us well to examine our role in the events that caused our hurt. Through honest self-examination, we uncover our part in the transgression.

Yet, in the heat of the moment, we are caught in the eye of the storm—blinded by resentment. To engage in true reflection, we must first find calm.

We realize our wrongs by connecting with our Higher Self, the spirit consciousness at the center of our being. We take full responsibility for our actions and forgive ourselves, sincerely desiring to refrain from such behavior.

If we conclude we were but innocent participants, we could ask, "What purpose does it serve me to hold on to this bitterness? Does it help me justify my loneliness, my anger or negative behavior?" Resentment serves no good purpose. It serves only to tear down our Divine Spirit.

Having forgiven ourselves, we are now ready to extend that same grace to others. When we commit to forgiveness, present resentments lose their hold on us, and future ones become mere irritations.

Forgiveness opens the door to empathy and compassion, softening our hurt and lifting our spirits.

November 25

Compliance and Acceptance

The mind complies, and the spirit accepts.

Early in life, we learn to comply as a way to avoid punishment. In this way we learn discipline and avoid consequences.

This logic does not apply to those who suffer from addictions. Addiction has serious consequences, and while an addict may wish to change course, the disease often lasts years for some and a lifetime for others.

In recovery, compliance may work for a time, but to ensure long-term sobriety, we must come to honestly accept our affliction and be consistent in our daily spiritual practice. The insidiousness of addiction is such that a weak link in our process weakens our resolve and threatens our state of recovery.

Consistency is the key to transforming our compliance into grateful acceptance.

November 26

Turning The Other Cheek

"Turning The Other Cheek" is not to be taken literally, but rather as a philosophy to ensure continued inner peace.

In times of conflict, we can assess what is most important: satisfying our volatile ego or harboring serenity. Rarely are there circumstances in which a hurt needs rise to the level of resentment, yet there are times when confrontation of a wrong is unavoidable. Even here we can be calm in our response, careful not to project harmful retaliation.

When we are upset, we bring the circumstance to our Higher Power and ask to be relieved of resentment by practicing calmness. The alternative is to create inner and outer conflict. If our goal is to live in peace, we must practice calm in our actions and thoughts.

When we retaliate or harbor resentment, we shut out the Spirit and lose inner peace. When we turn the other cheek, we practice healing, acceptance, and forgiveness and experience serenity.

November 27

Defining Our Priorities

We are taught that our family, responsibilities, and friends should take priority in our lives. With this in mind, where does self-care come in? Should our well-being not come first? Are we not taught to "put on our mask before helping others"? Without self-care, we cannot fulfill our expected roles.

All beings benefit from stepping away from earthly demands and having space to connect with themselves through self-reflection, hobbies, socialization or spiritual practice. Caring for ourselves is not selfish—it's essential for our well-being.

Our individual mental, physical, and spiritual care strengthens our resolve to become more loving and compassionate family members, increases our effectiveness in fulfilling our responsibilities, and deepens our friendships.

When we practice balance, we can do both, taking care of ourselves and fulfilling our defined priorities.

November 28

Joyful Silence

Our Higher Power graces us with Joyful Silence!

We speak of happiness, we speak of peace—but the meaning of our words has shifted throughout our lives.

What brought happiness to the child, the teenager, the young adult, the addict, the husband, the friend, and the father had varying degrees of joy. Time has passed, the old hats no longer fit, but each chapter has made its contribution to present day conditions.

The happiness and peace I experience now are found in moments where stillness exists—both in my external world and my inner spirit. The monkey mind reacts to an unpredictable world, but unlike the past, its call goes unanswered. Today, my natural spiritual state is one of calm.

Neutrality is a state of being that does not require action. Instead, it supports a diminished need for control and offers no resistance to the inevitable.

In moments of Joyful Silence, I experience peace and happiness.

.

November 29

Loneliness

Loneliness is real

Sorrow runs deep

Without the distraction of social interaction, I am alone with my restless mind. My life has changed drastically, and while I welcome the solitude, my mind alone cannot comfort me. Some feel this loneliness even amid a crowd.

But I have a Spiritual Companion who does not allow for extended periods of self-pity. In the silence of prayer and meditation, the love of an ever-present God of my understanding replaces loneliness and sorrow.

The mind interprets solitude as abandonment when social engagement is lacking.

Yet, distraction offers no real substance.

The spirit, however, welcomes silence as an opportunity for reflection.

Emotions ebb and flow; the presence of God, as we understand him, offers lasting permanence.

November 30

Feelings Are Not Facts!

Feelings are not facts. They are inner interpretations or reactions to external threats. We become vulnerable when our emotional comfort zone is threatened. Since I am powerless over that which exists beyond me, I strengthen that which exists within.

Our defense is based on self-knowledge and spiritual knowledge. Self-knowledge leaves little room for being ambushed by unexpected feelings. Thus, external circumstances and their effects are understood and more easily accepted.

Spiritual knowledge affords us insight into reality, humility to accept it as Truth, and a sincere expectation of a positive outcome.

When I am challenged by delusional perception, if I have established a solid spiritual defense, my thoughts and feelings will be ready and less likely to trigger inner turmoil.

Feelings are not facts!

December 1

We Do Recover

The mind may be tarnished but the spirit remains pure.

Being recovered from the disease of addiction means that we are no longer slaves to mental or behavioral compulsion. True recovery comes when the mind is cleansed, and the spirit finds clarity.

Cleansing of the mind implies that Truth overpowered denial granting us awareness of the causes and damage of our dependence, and preparing us to address our malady.

Clarity of spirit arises when we recognize what has protected our hearts from breaking and surrender to the guidance of a power greater than ourselves

We remain vigilant against deception, and with a clear mind—guided by the light of the spirit, we move forward, living a meaningful sober life.

December 2

A Return to Hell

To sustain recovery from addiction, I must remain abstinent from the source that triggered the compulsion, or I am guaranteed a return to hell.

We developed an allergy from which we are in remission. Sustained, intense displeasure is often a warning sign that we've entered Relapse Mode. This emotional state takes hold when we're deeply dissatisfied with our current circumstances—and if left unchecked, it often precedes the first drink or drug, a shopping spree, a food binge, a seat at the card table, or even an angry outburst.

The malady is of the spirit, and addiction is but a symptom. By returning to chemicals or past behaviors, we inevitably awaken old patterns and states of mind. We will again rely on a deceitful mind for guidance, for spirit coils from delusion. To avoid further consequences, we must quickly cut off its life supply and reach for the recovery tool kit to avoid relapse.

With constant vigilance and honest intent, we heed the warning signs and thus experience uninterrupted long-term sobriety and avoid a return to hell!

December 3

Recovered Sanity

Powerlessness over substances and the unmanageability of maladaptive behaviors are not temporary states. They remain dormant only as long as we maintain abstinence, for the disease is permanent. A pickle can never become a cucumber again. This allergy has a remedy but no cure. There is no vaccine to protect against recurrence, which can be fatal—or worse, a lifelong curse.

I do not fear relapse, but I am on high alert. The disease is cunning, baffling, and powerful. I have recovered my sanity; to remain in a state of recovery requires daily maintenance of my spiritual condition.

I avoid people, places, and things that threaten my sobriety by setting off an irreversible chain of events that could lead to relapsing to a previous way of existence.

Miracles are rare. To experience two in one lifetime is highly unlikely.

December 4

Adapting to Darkness

We adapt well to the path we can see;
We look ahead and prepare for the obstacles that lie before us. When we look back, we find clarity in where we've been and gratitude for the challenges we've overcome.

Make good of the light for it awakens insight.
Make there your most challenging choices.

Adapting to darkness is a fragment of human nature.
Fear thrives most where it remains hidden from the light.

Heed the warnings of the dark, for here we are to slow our pace. Small steps bring no fear. Darkness is time's offering for us to pray, ponder, reflect, dance with hurt, and wait for there to be light once more.

The unknown is of our creation. While I don't prescribe to the idea of a predestined outcome, I do believe that we can listen for Divine Guidance and in doing so, darkness no longer warrants my worry.

December 5

The Lost Sheep

Life compelled me to experience different herds. I quickly assimilated into each without needing direction, finding it easiest to follow the crowd.

Since my fellow travelers did not question the direction we were going in, I foolishly assumed that they knew the way. I followed blindly and without question, but an underlying sense of not belonging was always with me.

Eventually, I found myself lost and alone. I had become a lost sheep. Wounded by spiritual hunger and shivering cold, I spied a flock in the distance. Anywhere was a better place to be, so I joined them. I immediately felt a sincere kinship. Perhaps it was because I was no longer self-conscious; as we were all lost sheep in this group. I had found a home.

A watchful shepherd cared for our flock, leading us away from treacherous paths. We welcomed his guidance on a journey of daily spiritual nourishment. The shepherd kept the group intact while allowing for individuality.

I was lost, but now I'm found. I will follow the guidance of the Good Shepherd, for with Him, I will graze in fields of serenity and peace.

What if there was no shepherd? How would we know of love?

December 6

Shine the Light

Our spiritual malady grew in darkness. The dawn awakened the light of our soul.

Life moves in cycles, with inevitable peaks and valleys. Our challenge is not to resist them, but to learn to adapt and flow. Euphoria and despair, though opposites, are both states that cloud my vision of reality. The light of the spirit reveals my true balance. Yet this balance fades when I drift away from prayer.

Attachment is our quandary. Letting go is our solution.

Let go of earthly expectations and projections, for these hinder the process of our spiritual growth. Become free from the opinions of others; allow them in your midst, but do not allow their judgments, nor be judgmental yourself, for these block the light from shining on our tolerance and humility.

Disease grows in darkness. In the light, we find healing.

December 7

Accepting My Wrong

True acceptance lies in owning the wrongs I've committed, even when I long to blame another. The weight of that acceptance grows heavier as the wrongs grow more grievous.

When I was angry or hurt, my instinct was to find the culprit that caused my dejection. This mindset, which was my only coping skill to combat dis-ease, only fueled my addiction. My perceived injustices justified my need to escape the horrible infractions I endured in a world that seemed to unfairly single me out.

With my sanity restored, I came to accept that in the many dramatic events of my life, although circumstances and individuals changed, I was the common thread that connected them. While doing my inventory, I identified my wrongdoing in each situation. I, forgave myself, but only after deep, intentional repentance and whenever possible, making restitution for my actions toward the innocent participants and hostages I held during my years of active addiction.

Acceptance and responsibility do not come naturally—they come as a result of the daily practice of honesty and humility to the best of my ability. Acceptance of my wrongs provides release from the guilt and shame of a past that, once understood, strengthens my present moral resolve.

December 8

Giving Testimony

Sharing our testimony with others releases what has kept our spiritual path in darkness, for the burden of secrets keeps us spiritually sick.

Although we may wish to be thorough in our cleansing, we may intentionally or innocently omit certain events from our past. We do not deceive ourselves with justification.

To fully access the guidance of our Spiritual Guide, we must first cultivate willingness. Then, with complete honesty, we confess our immorality—first to another, then to our innermost self—and finally, we lay all past harm at the feet of our Great Friend.

In this way, we will live in the light of a glorious vision.

December 9

Self-Forgiveness

If we take the time to inventory ourselves, we will discover character flaws that we need to amend.

We will want to change the character trait that have us be short with our partner, inappropriately sarcastic to a friend or colleague, or the one that places blame on someone else for an act of our responsibility. We have a choice: bury our heads in the sand and pretend we are blameless or take responsibility for our actions.

Hurt people, hurt people! When we forgive ourselves—for all the things we should have done but didn't, and for all the things we did but should have refrained from—we free ourselves from the grip of guilt. Only then, reconciled with our wrongs, can we take true ownership of our deeds and sincerely commit to our Higher Self to avoid repeating those mistakes.

It's humbling to realize our human frailty and to accept that we regularly hurt others and ourselves. We mend our character through self-forgiveness and strong dedication to eliminating hurtful behaviors.

December 10

Moral Accountability

When we uncover character flaws during our inventory, we are called to treat them with patience and spiritual diligence. By acknowledging our negative traits with honesty and asking our Higher Power for help in eliminating them, we'll begin to see improvements in our attitudes and behaviors.

When we ask our Higher Power to help us limit our suffering by detaching from self-serving conduct, we awaken our innermost self—the source of spiritual guidance.

Yet, as we walk this path, temptation may arise to resurrect old behaviors, especially when we feel out of step with a society that does not hold itself to the same ethical standards. However, understanding that this disconnection exists because we travel in opposite directions is key, and it is not a reflection of us.

We care for our spiritual wellbeing through moral accountability.

December 11

Recovered Dignity

As our character finds its righteous path, we regain perspective on our faults. We no longer become defensive, nor do we question motives or doubt our every action. The way forward is to live our Truth. This depends entirely on our conscious acceptance of Higher Will.

We fear not criticism or judgment, for we enter all decisions guided by the light of spirit. Although our rough edges remain ever present in our daily dealings, we do not allow them a voice, for we have regained our dignity.

When our human path runs parallel to our spiritual path, separate but in unison, traveling with the same intention, we avoid repeating the regrettable of the past and live our lives with honest sincerity.

December 12

Cleansing

We do not allow what cannot be cleansed to disturb our peace. Yet, some remorse lingers for a lifetime, serving as a reminder of the ongoing inner reparation.

With the hurt we caused now far behind us, why must we still carry its cross today? Because hurt can be forgiven, but it is not forgotten. We release it only when we detach from the conscious mind.

Hurt cannot exist in the peacefulness of our inner temple—a sanctuary built on the foundation of meditation, with prayer as its walls and a roof gifted by the God of our understanding to protect us from inclement thoughts. This is the sacred space where our formal moments with the Divine unfold.

In the moments when we are engaged in sincere spiritual practice, our cleansing is granted.

December 13

The Shield of Faith

There are many times in the early hours of the morning when hopelessness and despair try to rob me of my serenity. It becomes a tug of war in which my faith is undefeated so far. It is a very real battle that cannot be minimized, for if I become weak, they will beckon my surrender.

Faith is precarious and without daily spiritual practice it is weakened. Time for reflection, whether through an inspirational reading, prayer and meditation, journaling, a recovery meeting, a walk in nature, physical exercise, or an informal conversation with my Higher Power, sustains my faith.

I need to remain consistent in my spiritual practice so that I am spiritually prepared to hold up The Shield of Faith and protect my serenity by transforming hopelessness into optimism and despair into spiritual calm.

December 14

Opting to Pray

The concept of prayer may seem complex. The process is unique to each individual, unfolding in different ways and at its own pace. There is no right or wrong way to go about praying.

Prayer is the act of entering a silent union with a Higher Power of our understanding. It can take the form of a dedicated moment at a specific time or a conscious effort to remain in communion throughout the day. At its core, prayer is a sincere desire to connect with and receive guidance from a Spiritual Source.

More important than our rituals is the outcome of our prayer. Through prayer, we harmonize with our personal Spiritual Friend. In the moments when we feel alone, and no human power can help us, our Friend is present to comfort us.

Prayer may have always been a part of our lives, or it may emerge from the depths of despair and loneliness.

Regardless of the time or way we pray, we will encounter the gentle touch of the Divine Force.

December 15

The Way of Sobriety

Just as a duckling trusts its mother hen and learns to care for itself, so too in early sobriety, we best stay close to the fellowship and allow for guidance. For us to develop false confidence and set out on our own proves perilous.

Those who have tested and proven safe this new way of living provide our initial set of directions. We take our first necessary steps by understanding and practicing basic moral principles. While we may grow to become expert climbers, we must never completely let go of the safety rope.

As we implement these new lifelines, we begin to gain the spiritual understanding they were meant to cultivate. When we become adept at interpreting the messages from our inner spirit, we are ready to venture out—allowing ourselves to loosen our grip on the rope of survival.

We maintain our sobriety by doing what was done for us, finding purpose in our service to others with guidance from our Higher Power.

This is the way of sobriety!

December 16

Allowing for Guidance

"God does for me what I cannot do for myself"

When I first heard this phrase, I was puzzled. I interpreted it as a religious statement that had nothing to do with how I understood the world. But now I realize that my confusion stemmed from the fact that I had not yet opened my eyes to the realm of the spirit and the natural order of the universe.

It seems that we have a lot of control over the conditions of our lives. In reality we have only the power of effort. Ultimately, our journey depends on others and circumstances. Once we accept this, we realize how small we really are.

Others and circumstances significantly influence the outcome of our daily lives. They are the ocean of which we are but a small wave. They play a part in everything we do and in creating all outcomes.

Rewording the original statement to "Others and circumstances do for me what I cannot do for myself" helps me better understand its meaning and increases my willingness to allow for guidance from Good Orderly Direction.

December 17

Searching for Completeness

Each day brought earthly complications. Just as the sun was about to smile from behind a cloud, another cloud would block its rays. I spent my life tirelessly searching for something to fill the void within—for whatever would finally make me feel complete. There were fleeting moments of calm, only to be followed by the disappointment of another failed attempt.

I sought completeness through earthly desires—whether material, relational, or tied to status. But these are flawed solutions, for there is always another possession to get, a more perfect relationship to chase, or another rung on the ladder of success to climb.

I did not feel whole until I found Spiritual Wealth. It has given me the gift of gratitude for all that I have. The light of the spirit has the ability to shine brightly through the thickest cloud.

Being thankful for people, things, and opportunities hasn't made my life perfect, but it has made me spiritually whole.

December 18

The Tiny Flame

At a time when my life was in complete disarray and had begun to lose all meaning, the Universe entrusted me with the care of a Tiny Flame. I felt unprepared for such a responsibility. The flame was pure light, pure love.

As I struggled to keep from falling apart and the malady grew within my spirit it was this Tiny Flame that kept the hope alive that one day I would find courage. Every time I held this angel in my arms, I felt his unconditional love and inner peace. At the time I felt unworthy of such a blessing.

I learned many lessons from this angel, who was sent to teach me honesty, courage, respect, love, and patience. With his message delivered, the flame has moved on. Even eternal flames and the innocence of angels must work through their imperfections and find their own way— to grow, to love, to face and overcome suffering and to learn from it all. Today, I believe I too have shed some light on his journey.

I am fully aware that his arrival was the most significant day of my life, closely followed only by my rebirth in recovery—for together, they comprise My Purpose on this earthly journey. As my living blessing completes another turn around the sun, he continues to bring kindness, devotion, and love to those he encounters.

Happy Birthday, son, and thank you for all your teachings, past and present.

December 19

Spiritual Survival

History teaches that all living organisms become territorial and self-serving to ensure their survival—except for martyrs and holy men, who have given themselves for the universe's greater good.

Leaving spiritual imprints on our journey does not require martyrdom. We can give to others with loving intention and compassionate action through small but significant acts. These benevolent acts sustain the survival of our spirit, for goodwill, mindful deeds, and offerings of peace, nourish it.

Let us open our territorial hearts each day and share of ourselves so that we, too, contribute to the greater good, not through martyrdom, but through our loving, peaceful intention that all feel welcomed by the open borders of our soul. In this way, we ensure our Spiritual Survival.

December 20

Purpose

There is a purpose to our lives and our purpose gives significance to our existence. Otherwise we would wander aimlessly without meaning or direction. Believing this, we then set ourselves the task of finding our purpose.

Our purpose is not found in grand accomplishments, but rather in simple roles assigned to us by the Divine Planner: being a son, a parent, a loving partner, a worker among workers, a sponsor, a caregiver, or a friend. No one can define or direct us toward our purpose. When we live in sync with our Higher Power, we will intuitively know our destined mission.

Once found, we must not minimize the importance of our intended purpose; it is unique to our execution and will go without satisfaction if not for our doing. No one purpose is of greater importance than another.

The Divine Planner asks only that we honestly try our very best to fulfill our spiritual mission. For the love, care, and devotion we put into our efforts, we will be rewarded with blessings and joy of having lived a meaningful existence.

December 21

An Open Channel

To experience Spirit, we must become an open channel through which it manifests. We do this naturally and, to some extent subconsciously when surrounded by nature.

When we gaze in awe at the rounded ridges of a high mountain, a seemingly endless ocean, or a luminous full moon, we realize how small we are in comparison. Lest we forget, we, too, are a part of this magnificent creation, guided by Universal Intelligence.

The mountain, the ocean, the moon and humanity are one. Together we contribute to the wholeness of this earthly experience. Becoming an open channel begins with the simple acceptance that we are not the center, that there is a power greater than us at work in the world.

We become an open channel when we accept that we are connected through Spirit to this great power. It is through this acceptance that we allow for spiritual guidance, much like the other wonders of nature.

December 22

Nature and Spirit

The laws of nature direct our path to mental and physical well-being. The laws of the spirit serve to guide our earthly journey. They bring deeper meaning to our experiences that would otherwise not be fully understood.

To better benefit from mental and physical health, we watch for delusional thinking, follow a healthy diet, and exercise.

To improve our spirit, we devote time to communing with our Higher Power through prayer and meditation.

While in nature, we judge good and bad, in the realm of the spirit, there are only lessons to help us understand both our joy and our suffering.

To maximize our human experience, we will want to follow the laws of nature while allowing for spiritual guidance. Both are essential to the wholeness of our human experience.

December 23

Inner Peace

Inner peace is the answered call to unconditional love.

At the core of earthly existence is love and peace. Yet, throughout time, this core has been misrepresented by the few who use deceptive rhetoric to gain power and create war in the name of justice or prosperity. As a people we must unite to influence and bring about world peace.

We contribute to outer peace by first creating inner peace. We strive for all that is good and accept the results of our best efforts. Inner peace arises when we accept forgiveness and understanding of ourselves, and with purity of heart, cultivate compassion and unconditional love for all others.

We must hold true that if we live this way, and long before we master self-love, our inner peace will create a ripple effect of compassion, if only in our small corner of the world.

December 24

Our Love

During this time of year, the world grows increasingly hurried and agitated, causing collective anxiety and stress to reach their peak. This is a natural response to an unnatural season that disrupts our lives—but only once a year. Amid the chaos, we would do well to pause and remember the true meaning of the season: to celebrate the birth of the one who came to embody peace, love, forgiveness, and humility.

Our restlessness often stems from the pressure to meet our expectations and those of others. We ask ourselves: What gift should I buy? Will they like it? Did I spend too much—or not enough? Is there enough food? Will someone feel hurt because they weren't invited?

Should we experience any of these discomforts, we can detach from the present moment, pause and reflect with gratitude for all the blessings our Higher Power has bestowed upon us. We can also offer a sincere prayer for so many who know only suffering.

Through intentions of kindness, may we increase tolerance and acceptance of ourselves and others, and embody the humility that this season was always meant to represent.

Our love cannot be tied with ribbons or placed beneath the tree. It is a gift to be given freely—every day, to everyone.

December 25

Yeshua

For most, this is a day of celebration—a time when families come together and gift one another. We celebrate the birth of a loving man that walked this earth thousands of years ago and whose teachings we've been taught but rarely follow.

Some will over-gift with meaningless objects that will soon find their way to the waste basket, while others will practice gluttony at the family gathering. Not far away, someone is suffering the pangs of hunger.

Many of our brothers and sisters will not have gifts to give or to receive; others are embroiled in violent wars, addiction, loneliness, hunger, disease, or homelessness. For those less fortunate, let's bow our heads and honor them with a prayer of hope and intention that perhaps the world will find a realistic solution to end their human suffering.

Let us remember the powerful message that Yeshua delivered to us, which is as relevant today as it was when He first delivered it. That we must love, cherish and uplift one another above all else.

On this holy day, as on all the days of your journey, I wish you all peace.

December 26

Spiritual Blessings

Living a spiritually principled life sometimes requires forgoing earthly rewards. We take our place in line, and when it's our turn, we receive what is rightfully ours. We are not cunning, manipulative, or dishonest in trying to gain an unfair advantage over others.

As a result, we may not always achieve our desired outcome when we want to—but rather, when it's meant to happen. Yet, the true benefit of living by spiritual principles is far greater: we are spared the stain of deceit and the heavy burden of carrying inner shame and greed.

Principled living often rewards us in ways beyond our understanding. Our desired outcomes may arrive in their own time, or they may not come at all, because a greater blessing awaits us elsewhere.

Living by moral principles challenges the logic of earthly desires. To choose a principled life is to seek spiritual blessings, which sometimes requires sacrificing worldly rewards.

December 27

Freedom or Misery

Addiction is a matter of life or death, freedom or misery.

The misery of addiction lies in the daily madness of chasing the "normal" when the highs are long gone and only the lows remain. We continue to use because it has become our relief, our escape from a world of our own making that traps us in unbearable grief and shame. The result is a slow, painful, spiritual death.

Freedom comes to those who want it, not to those who need it. It comes wrapped as a gift of desperation, for few seek what to them is the still unfamiliar concept of recovery.

Recovery is life. It is the freedom to choose how we want to live without the insane chatter of our compulsions. It is the feeling of finding belonging after years of living on the outskirts of society. Recovery is the life preserver that keeps us afloat, preventing us from inevitably drowning

Willingness is the small opening through which grace slips in, allowing an addict to choose freedom over misery and life over spiritual death.

December 28

Recovery Has a Sequence

Life follows a sequence. Recovery does too—a logical set of steps that promotes growth and leads us to stability. Yet, we often want to skip some of them, believing they don't apply to us. This is a mistake. Ignoring the instructions is what led to our impairment.

Our progress depends on our ability to surrender to the process. By surrendering our will and taking suggestions, we gain a sober life. Do not rush, for this is not a race, nor is there a final destination. All that exists is the priceless now.

We celebrate our sobriety today, for tomorrow remains uncertain. Follow the sequence, read the instructions, and remain open to guidance.

Take the suggestions. they are free; you will only pay for the ones you ignore.

December 29

Sharing Optimism

I am a product of my thoughts and actions. Positive energy creates positive results. When I share my optimism with others, my rewards double. I cannot give what I do not have, so my impact on others is as fruitful as my commitment to my personal growth.

My optimism depends on my state of mind. When acceptance, tolerance, and gratitude guide my thoughts, I eliminate negative thinking, the root cause of worry and fear, and increase positivity.

Spiritual prosperity grows only through daily prayer and meditation, which cultivates clarity of thought. With clear thinking and a heart full of optimism, we model right action and inspire others to create change in the areas of their lives where they feel unfulfilled.

Sharing our optimism may motivate others, but our greatest reward is our commitment to service.

December 30

Grace of Spirit

One cannot pretend to know the grace of a spiritual life without first opening a heart free of judgment and removing the blindfold of prejudice.

Once we do, the miraculous power of the Spirit is limited only by the strength of our faith.

When we willingly surrender delusion, the Spirit brings about a strong mind. We must not confuse Truth with desire, for desire alone does not allow faith to cross the threshold of our soul.

The grace of the Spirit lightens our overburdened minds, for in the knowledge of Truth, our vision becomes clear and unbiased.

December 31

On The Last Day

On the last day, I will wake up in our quaint country cottage, immersed in love and surrounded by nature. A sense of peaceful well-being will permeate my soul. There will be animals, gardens, and the resounding sounds of birds. A lazy river may give way to the soft whisper of a gentle cascading waterfall.

My heart in anticipation of the mystery that awaits my arrival, will be filled with love for those who cherish me, forgiveness for those who have caused me hurt, acceptance for life's joys, and gratitude for the sufferings that accelerated my growth. My most precious treasure will be my bond, dependence, and obedience to the Spiritual Source.

On my final day, everything will be left behind—material objects will no longer hold purpose. My only desire is to depart this life embraced by the grace and peace of the Master of Unlimited Power, Wisdom, and Love.

Index

Absolved, 127, **Abstinence**, 129, 160, 338 **Abstinence vs sobriety**, 126, 210 **Acceptance,** 12, 17, 25, 28, 31, 32, 42, 53, 56, 59, 62, 68, 74, 77, 78, 90, 103, 110, 116, 117, 124, 127, 135, 161, 168, 174, 214, 215, 216, 222, 235, 243, 247, 255, 261, 273, 277, 285, 286, 293, 294, 299, 313, 330, 331, 342, 346, 364,366 **Accountable**, 132, 161, 205, 345 **Acknowledge,** 109, 219, 242, 285 **Action**, 47, 53, 62, 84, 123, 160, 199, 202, 265, 303, 364 **Actor,** 20, 184 **Addict**, 160, 290, 292, 362 **Addiction,** 54, 59, 74, 89, 94, 99, 117, 120, 129, 151, 187, 213, 281, 287, 291, 326, 330, 336, 342, 362 **Admission**, 93 **Adult-child** , 175 **Adversity,** 77 **Aligning our will,** 70, 83, 111, 116, 196, 255 **Allergy** , 337 **Alter reality,** 271, 317 **Alternative life style,** 326 **Altruism,** 79 **Amends,** 96, 109, 124, 127, 176 **Angel,** 190 **Anger** , 23, 41, 45, 63, 64, 66, 91, 100, 122, 123, 134, 141, 151, 167, 207, 213, 242, 268, 291 **Anonymity,** 74 **Anticipation,** 366 **Anxiety,** 64, 94, 359 **Approval, Need for,** 26, 127, 176, 248, 264, 287, 314 **Arrogance,** 63, 64, 153, 240, 248, 269, 270, 292, 314 **Attachment,** 35, 128, 155, 246, 341 **Attitude,** 110, 218, 243 **Authentic,** 144, 203, 269, 282, 327 **Avoidance,** 15, 82, 85, 238, 279 **Awakened,** 14, 19, 26, 27, 38, 95, 115, 132, 147, 151, 218, 223, 252, 287, 312   , 339, 341 **Awareness** , 33, 36, 61, 80, 82, 86, 93, 99, 105, 111, 113, 123, 127, 148, 176, 199, 223, 260, 268, 271, 273, 278, 300, 301 **Baffled** , 78, 114 **Balance,** 79, 82, 106, 111, 125, 147, 150,, 175, 299, 341 **Be,** 318 **Beginners,** 323 **Being,** 7, 72, 168, 172, 186, 195, 252 **Belief,** 10, 11, 68, 82, 95, 110, 112 **Belief,** 157, 161, 304, 316, 328 **Belief system,** 51 **Benefit others,** 102 **Benevolent,** 354 **Betrayal,** 44, 107, 141, 266, 287, 326 **Beyond Wildest dreams,** 126 **Blame,** 44, 127, 132, 164, 176, 212, 256, 342 **Blessings,** 35, 36, 49, 87, 117, 126, 229, 231, 280, 353, 359, 361 **Blocks to Recovery,** 208 **Bondage of self,** 101 **Bottom, Hitting,** 90, 93, 178, **Boundaries** , 97, 121, 282 **Brain chemistry,** 177 **Buddha,** 16 **Burnout,** 305 **Calm,** 16, 22, 41, 77, 84, 91, 98, 131, 136, 164, 169, 230, 318, 331 **Capacity,** 60, 67, 123 **Challenges,** 28, 67, 76, 78, 112, 126, 142, 235, 315, 323 **Change,** 14, 19, 49, 53, 60, 71, 127, 151, 159, 170, 176, 218, 247, 327 **Channel,** 50, 57, 136, 320, 356 **Character,** 28, 41, 57, 64, 99, 101,155, 172, 219, 238, 244, 250, 344, 346 **Character assassination,** 265 **Character defect,** 105, 218, 244, **Character flaws,** 13, 103, 291, 344, 345 **Character traits,** 63, 132, 247, 224 **Charitable,** 108, 130, 155, 173 **Choice,** 15, 28, 36, 42, 57, 61, 70, 82, 88, 153, 162, 260, 293, 339 **Choice (not),** 187, 290 **Civilians,** 168 **Clarity,** 57, 59, 109,

144, 151, 154, 199, 200, 212, 214, 223, 275, 339, 364 **Cleansing**, 103, 217, 236, 343, 347 **Coincidence**, 76, 116, 139 **Come to Believe**, 60 **Comfort**, 22, 119, 137, 143, 165 **Commitment**, 59, 109, 113, 166, 170, 215, 220 **Commitment**, 268, 300, 364 **Communication**, 40, 44, 287 **Communion, with HP**, 28, 50, 86, 111, 136, 214, 219, 234, 247, 313, 323 **Compare**, 20, 73, 85, 321 **Compassion**, 35, 71, 81, 91, 96, 106, 107, 121, 123, 134, 138, 155, 167, 224, 247, 256, 258, 263, 265, 266, 300, 329, 358 **Completeness**, 152, 180, 352 **Compliance**, 330 **Compromise**, 128, 164, 287 **Compulsion**, 94, 102, 151, 244, 271, 337 **Conceit**, 63, 283 **Conscious-ness**, 113, 114, 135, 166, 177, 192, 206, 242, 255, 308, 315 **Conditioning**, 85,132, 144, 147, 154, 297 **Confession**, 101, 103 **Confidence**, 67, 166, 315 **Conflict**, 28, 40, 83, 90, 129, 134, 182, 235, 252 **Conform**, 125, 175, 269 **Connection to a HP**, 4, 21, 38, 43, 52, 62, 129, 202, 261 **Conscious-ness**, 15, 16, 18, 67, 80, 89, 112 **Consequences** 15, 48, 55, 271, 290 **Consistency**, 86, 244, 323, 330, 348 **Contemplation**, 4, 39, 109, 171 **Contentment**, 135, 263 **Contradict the mind**, 47 **Control**, 34, 37, 39, 83, 97, 99, 120 **Control**, 181, 197, 248, 305, 351 **Conversion**, 117, 247, 353 **Courage**, 10, 30, 72, 80, 111, 147, 154, 179, 182, 217, 227, 229, 235, 273, 353 **Criticism**, 88, 163, 257, 346 **Crutch**, 273, 299 **Cues**, 80 Culture, 51, 87, 140, 183, 260, 295 **Cunning**, 183,361 **Cunning, Baffling, Powerful** 186, 338 **Cure**, 232, 250 **Cyclical**, 88, 169, 256151, 169, 235, 341 **Daily Reprieve**, 154 **Darkness**, 17, 43, 62, 110, 148, 153, 323, 339, 341 **Debacle**, 190, 208, 209, 211 **Deception**, 21, 89, 101, 140, 211, 263, 336 **Decision making**, 11, 51, 61, 309 **Defects traits**, 105, 244 **Defense Mechanisms**, 238, 247 **Delusion**, 7, 16, 20, 37, 41, 46, 50, 52, 57, 65, 67, 68, 84, 85, 90, 96, 103, 126, 137, 143, 166, 171, 183, 185, 188, 195, 213, 225, 234, 238, 255, 257, 261, 264, 273, 297, 312, 313, 315, 316, 323, 326, 365 **Denial**, 222, 238, 256, 336, 357 **Depression**, 94 **Desire**, 119, 123, 151, 194, 215, 218, 245, 296, 319, 325, 365 **Despair**, 22, 39, 63, 95, 131, 187, 200, 225, 226, 290, 348, 349 **Desperation**, 157, 237, 278, 284, 307, 362, 311 **Destiny**, 68, 70, 240, 316 **Distractions**, 150 **Destructive thinking**, 72 **Detach** , 16, 43, 61, 63, 64, 77, 84, 86, 98, 99, 134, 140, 223, 228, 255, 282, 295, 296, 345 **Devotion**, 50, 86, 113, 213 **Dignity**, 186, 187, 275, 290, 346 **Direction**, 19, 285, 340, 350 **Dis-ease**, 52, 99, 111, 117, 122, 178, 184, 188, 196, 198 , 244, 248, 261, 342 **Dis-honest**, 15 Disillusionment, 141 **Disappointment**, 6, 11, 72, 87, 100, 176 **Discipline**, 112, 170, 201, 220, 228, 236, 300, 330 **Discomfort** 228, 237, 272, 359 **Disease**,

110, 117, 186, 188, 232, 290, 336, 338 **Distraction**, 150, 255
Disturbance,50,95,149,194,249,313 **DIVINE:** 27, 52 **connection**,
129 **consciousness**, 149, 152, 156 **energy**, 24 **intervention**, 18, 68,
154, 156, 174, 213, 271, 316 **path**, 72 **quiet**, 21. **Doubt**, 19, 38, 39,
44, 57, 88, 95, 102, 149, 194, 204, 305, 307, 313, 328 **Dysfunction**,
15, 30 , 66, 88, 104, 120, 122 **EARTLHY:** (instinct/thinking), 43,
demands, 331 **experience**, 80 **instinct** , 91 **limitations,** 113, 325
rewards, 361 **thinking**, 43 **desires**, 325, 352, 361 **Effort**, 16, 49, 67,
88, 105, 115, 134, 242, 351 **Ego**, 15, 18, 28, 35, 37, 51, 52, 55, 57, 81,
102, 103, 152, 225, 250, 278, 331 **Embrace**, 46, 65, 198, 225, 246,
312 **Emotions**, 33, 34, 44, 50, 52, 85, 98, 112, 131, 135, 147, 148,
151, 175, 228, 242, 265 **Emotional Turmoil**, 62, 323 **Emotional
Survival**, 65 **Empathy**, 81, 123, 134, 141, 155, 163, 243, 256, 257,
300, 306, 329 **Empower**, 84, 323 **Emptiness**, 278 **Enable**, 233
Enlightenment, 78, 86, 193, 217, 225, 291 **Environment** 87
Envy, 16, 23, 45, 73, 92, 280 **Equality**, 71, 89 **Equilibrium**, 52, 98,
299 **Equinimity**, 130 **Escape**, 90, 147, 150, 151, 169, 190, 199, 249,
272, 362 **Essence**, 274 **Estrangement** 168 **Eternal Peace**, 23, 83,
182 **Euphoria**, 341 **Evil**, 45, 118, 154 **Exercise**, 62, 177, 357
Expectation, 26, 47, 54, 85, 96, 139, 140, 141, 176, 212, 215   ,
216, 255, 256, 282, 297, 307, 341, 359 **Experience strenght hope**,
205 **Experiences,** 91, 102, 148, 159, 161 **External Conditions**, 22,
26, 100, 104, 141, 293 **Failure,** 11, 78, 88, 96, 165, 205, 310 **Faith,**
10, 11, 12, 14, 21, 36, 38, 50, 51, 53, 61, 94, 104, 112, 118, 122, 137,
139, 156, 162, 169, 171, 216, 225 , 253, 263, 268, 277, 300, 303, 304,
310, 311, 328, 348 **False pride**, 20 **False Prophet**, 183, 184, 185,
186, 187, 188, 189, 190, 209 **Family**, 51, 87, 117, 140, 189, 360
Fantasy, 82, 153, 203 **Favor**, 149, 223 **Fear**, 7, 8, 11, 14, 19, 22, 37,
39, 44, 45, 51, 57, 66, 67, 69, 70, 85, 89, 94, 97, 112, 137, 169, 184,
208, 214, 234, 248, 268, 295, 310, 315, 339, 364 **Feelings,** 7, 12   ,
44, 111, 195, 265, 335 **Fellowship 12 step**, 162, 201, 229, 232, 250,
284 **Fertile soil**, 61, 89, 299 **Flexibility**, 210, 263 **Flow**, 14, 18, 31,
34, 70, 83, 116, 324 **Footprint**, 61, 254 **Forgiveness**, 12, 17, 28, 39,
40, 42, 91, 107, 109, 123, 127, 134, 151, 167, 176, 205, 210, 266, 268,
276, 287, 298, 329, 331, 344, 347, 358, 366 **Freedom**, 85, 94, 110,
117, 125, 154, 166, 175, 362 **Fulfillment**, 119, 175, 293, 307
Genuine, 75, 202, 207, 283, 302 **Gift of desperation**, 62, 137, 362
Gifts of Sobriety, 1, 28, 35, 46, 55, 58, 75, 79, 87, 226
God, 45, 51, 139, 196, 202, 205, 213, 230, 232, 240, 272, 317
320, 334, 351 **Golden child**, 184 **Good and evil**, 43 **Good guy**, 29,
198 **Good-bad**, 98, 231 **Grace**, 90, 186, 191, 214, 230, 268, 281, 286,

292, 327, 365, 366 **Grandiosity**, 64, 89, 92, 126, 138, 210, 253, 292 **Gratitude,** 1, 13, 25, 36, 42, 46, 48, 55, 59, 64, 69, 74, 76, 92, 104, 111, 117, 119, 122, 130, 135, 166, 210, 231, 266, 270, 280, 319, 321, 339, 359, 364, 366 **Greed**, 23, 37, 44, 52, 63, 69, 122, 174, 268, 321 **Grief,** 3, 101, 171, 182, 222, 299, 362 **Grievance**, 44, 244 **Growth,** 72, 327, 363, 364, 366 **Guidance,** 1, 4, 6, 9, 11, 17, 18, 34, 41, 43, 45, 49, 50, 68, 72, 76, 78, 82, 83, 84, 90, 98, 105, 106, 108, 111, 113, 116, 119, 120, 128, 130, 136, 137, 149, 152, 158, 179, 196, 197, 201, 211 213, 219, 223, 234, 236, 251, 273, 293, 309, 313, 316, 336, 340, 349, 350, 363 **Guilt** , 3, 48, 87, 94, 101, 107, 122, 124, 127, 132, 159, 167, 176, 178, 247, 291, 342 **Happiness**, 24, 48, 49, 74, 78, 79, 86, 87, 100, 119, 131, 142, 165, 196, 231, 237, 255, 280, 333, 344 **Harm**, 41, 107, 109, 167 **Harmony**, 4, 28, 69, 106, 121, 133, 152, 162, 252   , 298, 322 **Healing**, 20, 21, 47, 58, 59, 87, 102, 104, 110, 120, 129,131, 131, 144, 146, 152, 157, 161, 273, 275, 278, 290, 326, 331, 341 **Helplessness,** 34 **Hereafter** 276 **Higher power**, 1, 6, 12, 39, 55, 56, 60, 86, 99, 101, 107, 110, 111, 114, 115, 120, 122, 131, 142, 161, 162, 191, 194, 195, 196, 197, 201, 204, 206, 219, 230, 255, 258, 261, 275, 277, 309, 331, 357, 359 **Higher self**, 16, 31, 123, 254, 273, 300, 308, 309, 329, 344 **Higher thought**, 28 **Hijacking**, 189 **Honesty**, 15, 25, 30, 65, 75, 88, 99, 103, 164, 186, 197, 217, 285, 312, 330, 342, 343 **Honor**, 232 **Hope**, 1, 57, 60, 61, 94, 95, 110, 154, 190, 193, 194, 197, 201, 203, 208, 214, 216, 294, 303 **Hopelessness**, 93, 177, 178, 198, 348, **HUMAN: condition**, 250, 268 **doing-being**, 5, 85, 165, 252 **experience**, 1, 23, 48, 50, 54, 66, 71, 78, 83, 86, 231, 357 **frailty**, 344 **interaction**, 58 **nature**, 155, 270 **solution**, 169, 290 **Humanity**, 31, 52, 63, 141, 163, 165, 213, 215, 218, 243, 251, 307 **Humility**, 18, 24, 25, 29, 37, 40, 43, 56, 63, 64, 65, 69, 71, 74, 79, 81, 91, 92, 96, 99, 105, 124, 127, 138, 149, 155, 160, 161, 166, 172, 176, 205, 210, 215, 218, 219, 235, 255, 268, 273, 291, 292, 300, 312, 341, 344, 359 **Hurt**, 6, 22, 31, 33, 72, 91, 96, 131, 140, 155, 161, 167, 172, 176, 275, 344, 366 **Ideals**, 52, 161, 261, 267, 282 **Identification**, 44, 58, 101, 104, 162, 178, 326 **Ignorance**, 28 81, 153, 197, 305 **Illuminate**, 43 **Illusory**, 48, 74, 180 **Immediate gratification**, 74, 146, 228 **Impatience**, 146, 297 **Imperfections**, 20, 25, 32, 125, 194, 196, 248, 302, **Imposter**, 184, 188 **Impulsivity**, 55, 148, 177 **Individuality**, 20, 125, 145, 163, 295 **Inevitable,** 70, 305 **Inferiority**, 89, 248 **Injustice**, 41, 64, 299 **Inner calm** 45, 59, 77, 100, 111, 113, 155, 174, 175, 208, 223, 266, 279, 331, 353, 358 **Inner Child**, 50, 87, 121, 175 **Inner Conflict,** 293 **Inner self**, 16, 67, 122, 129, 165, 208, 225, 253, 294, 358 **INNER:**

solution, 156 **spirit,** 21, 22, 26, 64, 111, 122, 143, 149, 165, 234, 240, 249,350 **turmoil,** 19, 39, 48, 55, 91, 199, 293 **voice,** 179 **Innocence,** 85 121, 212 **Insanity,** 47, 90, 153, 154, 211, 261, 273, 278, 281, 311 **Insecurity,** 45, 69, 184 **Inside job,** 32, 74   **Insidious,** 170, 281 **Insight,** 32, 111, 127, 151, 159, 176, 212, 223, 235, 238, 260, 308, 330, **Inspiration,** 32, 57, 80, 96, 100, 106, 142, 245, 314, 327, 364 **Instant Gratification,** 146, 188, 196 **Instinct,** 18, 114, 293 **Integrity,** 71, 127, 140 **Intended,** 19, 67, 70, 76, 181, 293, 309 **Intended destination,** 14, 23, 24, 72, 116 **Intention,** 4, 21, 39, 43, 44, 111, 149, 158, 216, 258, 265, 270, 274, 286 **Intolerance,** 37, 134 **Intuition,** 114, 215, 286, 355 **Inventory,** 32, 37, 99, 101, 103, 109, 111, 130, 216, 218, 231, 270, 314, 344, 345 **Isolation,** 120, 166, 191, 195, 200, 323, 326 **Jeolousy,** 25, 52, 57, 66, 148, 174, 195, 213, 255, 265, 268, **Journey,** 87, 110, 146, 157, 166, 193, 194, 201, 204, 212, 216, 231, 239, 242, 300, 319, 324 **Judgement,** 16, 17, 20, 30, 37, 76 85, 88, 99, 101, 125, 127, 142, 163, 175, 182, 197, 212, 248, 255 256, 265, 272, 295, 341, 346, 357, 365 **Justice,** 39 **Justification,** 101, 124, 167, 225, 238, 291, 329, 342, 343, **Karma,** 292, 298 **Lessons,** 34, 41, 42, 43, 48, 61, 76, 88, 96, 123, 204, 250, 353 **Let Go Let God,** 310 **Letting go,** 46, 125, 181, 192, 310, 341 **Liberation,** 101, 103, 115, 192, 296, 298, 311 **Lie (the),** 261, 262 **Light,** 17, 27, 50, 51, 62, 95, 110, 148, 154, 157, 213, 226, 313, 339, 341 **Logic,** 47, 60, 82, 97, 117,156 157, 185, 192, 241, 273, 319, 330, 361, 362 **Loneliness,** 92, 178, 334, 349 **Lost sheep,** 340, **Love,** 12, 25, 45, 52, 57, 121, 155, 168, 212, 258, 266, 359, 360, 366 **Loyalty** , 71, 232 **Maintenance,** 170, 338, 350 **Maladaptive behavior,** 54, 159, 213, 238, 338, **Malady,** 89, 92, 94, 109, 112, 122, 129, 144, 189, 191, 196, 255, 268, 336, 341, 353 **Malice,** 25, 43, 44, 91, 107, 167, 227 **Manifestation,** 38, 158, 199 **Manipulative,** 15, 211, 302, 361 **Mask** , 20, 54, 65, 312 **Mastery** , 19 **Material – spiritual,** 43 **Material (realm/objects),** 34, 48, 49, 63, 69, 79, 86, 92, 100, 119, 126, 128, 136, 143, 144, 145, 171, 185, 279, 297, 324 **Maturity,** 161, **Meaningful life,** 71, 87, 355 **Meditation,** 16, 21, 53, 62, 113, 177, 206, 254, 283 **Meetings, 12 step,** 160, 162, 195, 201, 202, 203 **Memories,** 61, 305 **Mental Physical Spiritual** , 66, 332 **Mentor,** 205, 309 **Message** , 33, 80, 111, 174, 192, 194 **Message, carry,** 27, 58, 115, 81 **Mind the,** 14, 15, 21, 37, 39, 47, 82, 83, 86, 117, 122, 128, 150, 152, 159, 169, 177, 185, 220, 252, 262, 296, 317
Mind altering, 59, 89, 90, 122, 129, 169, 257, 275, 300
Mind body soul, 62, 66, 237 **Mindfulness,** 18, 235 **Minimize** 172, 348 **Miracle,** 57, 59, 60, 62, 72, 87, 94, 116, 117, 126, 156, 190, 192,

229, 275, 328, 365 **Misery,** 213, 253, 275, 362 **Mistakes,** 74, 124 **Model,** 168, 205, 266, 327 **Moderation** 190 **Mantra,** 228 **Moral,** 59, 172, 187, 196, 283, 314, 345 **Motivation,** 62, 88, 170, 237, 328 **Mourn,** 3, 17, 212 **Mystery,** 50, 70, 71, 102, 181, 206, 253 **Naturalspirit laws,** 78, 357 **Negativity,** 19, 59, 204, 228 **Neutrality,** 98, 165, 212, 319,333 **New Beginnings,** 1, 14, 166 **Newcomer,** 232, 326, 328 **Now, the**, 31, 36, 46, 67, 313 **Numbing,** 185 **Nurturing,** 121, 146, 150, 155 **Obedience,** 214, 366 **Obsessions,** 210, 211, 244 **Obstacle,** 23, 35, 58, 70, 111, 113, 143, 179, 186, 208, 250, 339 **One day at a time,** 8, 172, 209 **Open Mind** 197, 206 **Opinion of others,** 12, 125, 364 **Optimism,** 112, 250, 303, 364 **Origin,** 184 **Outcome,** 318, 351, 361 **Outcome,** 67, 82, 88, 164, 216, 304 **Outlook,** 10, 118, 231, 315 **Over Confidence,** 59 **Overcoming,** 70, 113, 125, 155, 189, 315 **Paralyzing,** 156, 169, 181, 304 **Parasite,** 186 **Parental influence,** 147, 260, 287, 302, 319 **Past,** 31, 72, 96, 124, 127, 159, 327, 346 **Patience,** 12, 25, 28, 50, 146, 172, 206, 218, 219, 235 **Peace,** 6, 16, 18, 36, 39, 49, 57, 66, , 88, 100, 227, 253, 255, 260, 333, 358, 366 **People places things,** 166, 181, 195, 338 **People pleaser,** 18, 20, 74, 302 **Perfect order** , 45, 83, 231 **Perfection,** 149, 291 **Personalities,** 155, 247, 272 **Perspective,** 42, 53, 84, 133, 141, 163, 176, 211, 243, 319 **Pessimism**, 118, 122, 177, 220, 250, 256, 303 **Pink cloud,**166 202 **Potential,** 245 **Powerless,** 34, 105, 197, 200, 335, 338 **Praise,** 73, 121 **Prayer,** 2, 36, 39, 49, 50, 53, 62, 64, 84, 107,109 132, 139, 204, 206, 158, 162, 176, 177, 195, 202, 266, 280, 283, 289, 341, 349, 360 **Prayer and meditation,** 113, 136, 160, 294 334, 348, 357, 364 **Pre-conditioned response,** 159 **Pre-destined,** 71, 339 **Prejudice,** 45, 265, 365 **Preparation** 11 **Present,** 242, 267, 315, 321 **Prestige,** 37, 126, 185, 216 **Pride,** 64, 89, 105, 248, 250, 251, 273, 291 **The Principles 214-221 Principles,** 15, 28, 37, 51, 71, 77, 81, 111, 115 , 26, 137, 155, 199, 214, 220, 221, 231, 232, 235, 244, 252, 361, 277, 279, 295, 300, 301, 350 **Priorities,** 106, 135, 236, 310, 326, 332 **Procrastination,** 59, 170, 177, 202, 251, 286, 304, 310 **Process (of recovery)** 87, 113, 117, 157, 179, 196, 233, 341 212, 215, 217, 218, 222, 224, 246, 247, 278, 290, 323, 330, 342, 363 **Productive,** 32 **Progress,** 111, 132, 196, 207, 218, 224, 239, 246, 363 **Projection,** 31, 148, 171, 215, 313, 341 **PROMISES: I,** 94, 195, **II,** 61, 96, 195 **III,** 98 **IV,** 100 **V,** 102 **VI,** 104 **VII,** 106 **VIII,** 108 **IX,** 110 **X,** 112 **XI,** 114 **XII,** 116 **Protection,** 49, 140, 214 **Providence,** 193, 281 **Psychological rewiring,** 129 **Punitive,** 91

From Delusion to Truth

Pure, 26, 31, 39, 44, 45, 51, 52, 7, 80, 87, 101, 121, 128, 157, 179, 180, 182, 270, 274, 286, 288, 290, 353, 358 **Purpose,** 11, 14, 32, 61, 71, 76, 87, 93, 96, 126, 142, 166, 174, 189, 200, 225, 236, 245, 254, 289, 300, 311, 322, 350 **Rambling thoughts,** 192 **Random (events)** 80 **Rationalization,** 16 **Re-condition mind,** 159 **Real self**, 54, 184, 312 **Reality,** 16, 30, 31, 36, 82, 90 101, 129, 144, 146, 183, 199, 211, 215, 216, 222, 263, 313, 324, 328, 351 **Rebel,** 83, 125, 145, 147, 287 **Reconciliation,** 145, 146 **Recovered,** 94 102, 146, 156, 232, 327, 336, 338 160 **Recovery,** 47, 59, 60, 62, 72, 87, 100, 102, 122, 126, 144, 151, 160, 170, 172, 193, 195, 199, 207, 209, 211, 227, 229, 232, 256, 283, 290, 300, 314, 362, 363 **Redemption,** 281, **Reflection,** 5, 22, 34, 100, 111, 143, 234 , 308, 332, 339, 348 **Reflections Anniv. Month** 183 – 213, **Refuge,** 54, 56, 162, 234, 272, 297, 319 **Regrets,** 3, 25, 42, 96, 124, 173, 182, 222, 292, 298, 346 **Reintegration,** 172 **Rejection,** 11, 30, 164 **Relapse,** 90, 256, 337, 338 **Relationship, with HP,** 53, 160, 316 **Relief,** 59, 66, 107, 151, 196, 212, 214, 323, 362 **Religion,** 25, 51, 295, 351 **Remorse,** 48, 131, 298, 347 **Reparation,** 99, 107, 109, 347 **Repent,** 25, 342 **Repress,** 148 **Reprieve (daily)** 154, 298 **Reputation,** 39, 63, 172, 292 **Resentment,** 16, 18, 23, 25, 33, 34, 37, 156, 41, 44, 52, 57, 64, 66, 77, 85, 87, 91, 96, 116, 146, 159, 164, 167, 172, 195, 207, 210, 213, 222, 234, 242, 243, 268, 286, 287, 293, 311, 319, 324, 331, 333, 336, 341 **Resilience,** 33, 48, 96, 146, 164, 204 **Resistance,** 34, 41, 64, 77, 116, 156, 243, 286, 287, 293, 311, 319, 324, 331, 333 , 341 **Resolution,** 72, 123, 164 **Respect,** 314, **Responsible,** 58, 67, 88, 103, 107, 109, 115, 123, 127, 201, 315, 344 **Restitution,** 342 **Restless Irritable Discontent,** 244, **Restlessness,** 28, 35, 69, 272, 359 **Restored** 90, 129, 172, 197 **Restraint,** 12, 41, 146, 265, 274 **Retaliation,** 167, 331 **Revenge,** 265 **Righteous,** 71, 75, 103, 244, 346 **Rigid,** 8, 40, 70, 147, 263, 295 297, 319 **Ripple,** 71, 75 **Risk,** 11, 14, 30, 80, 139, 147, 161, 164 **Ritual,** 5, 33, 202, 234, 239 **Role** , 30, 54 **Root cause,** 144   **Routine,** 220, 232, 297 **Running,** 19, 177, 264 **Sacrifice,** 86 **Saint Francis prayer,** 39, 48 **Salvation,** 95, 129, 342 **Sanity,** 90, 95, 129, 338, 342 **Script,** 54, 121, 260, 287 **Secret** , 217, 343 **Seductive,** 90 **Seeking guidance,** 112 **SELF: guidance,** 184 **actualization,** 65, 80, 125, 312 **centeredness,** 28, 55, 63, 65, 81, 88, 106, 107, 198, 199, 210, 232, 240, 248, 264, 268, 279, 283, 300 **confidence,** 19 **conscious,** 300, 340 **destructive,** 323 **direction,** 296 **doubt,** 140, 184, 300, 321 **esteem,** 20, 74, 321 **examination,** 123 **forgiveness,** 278, 298 **gratification,** 224 **importance,** 63,64, 269 **love,** 278, **reliance,** 213

respect, 189, 314 **seeking,** 236 **Serving,** 26, 108, 109, 185, 274, 345 **sufficient,** 92 **Will,** 64, 98, 321 **Self-pity,** 10, 13, 23, 37, 53, 61, 66, , 94, 101, 104, 177,178, 188, 190, 211, 213, 242, 250, 291, 299, 303, 323, 334 **Selfish** 11, 13, 43, 81, 106, 134, 172, 176, 218, 225, 231, 240, 256, 53, 279 298 **Selfless,** 11, 13, 27 , 36, 40, 43, 53, 61, 63, 64, 66, 79, 94, 101, 106, 157, 161, 172, 173, 174, 177, 210, 211, 213, 218, 225, 231, 232, 234, 242, 250, 256, 268, 278, 279, 287, 288, 298, 300, 304, 314, 323, 334 **Sequence,** 128, 363 **Serenity,** 9, 18, 22, 36, 41, 46, 43, 56, 59, 62, 75, 85, 98, 112, 135, 167, 190, 212, 214 253, 287, 313, 331 **Serenity prayer,** 135, 204, 213, 215, 299, 319 **Servant,** 63, 64, 160, 194, 300 **Service,** 41, 62, 75, 96, 111 160, 162, 224, 225, 350, 364 **Shadow, my,**148 **Shame,** 65, 66, 85, 87, 99, 107, 131, 140, 148, 159, 164, 167, 178, 184, 188, 217 247, 291, 342, 361 **Sharing,** 13, 104, 154, 195, 281, 323, 364 **Short comings,** 32, 78 , 283, 302 **Showing up,** 15, 67, 166, 201, 285, 315 **Significance,** 355 **Silence,** 44, 333 **Simplicity,** 60, 69, 97, 98, 156, 194, 270, 286, 317 **Sincere** ,15, 26, 30, 38, 50, 86, 123, 218, 346, 347 **Sins,** 49, 127, 292 **Situations,** 143 **Sobriety,** 62, 103, 166, 194, 196, 209, 330, 326, 336, 338, 350, 363 **Social status,** 144 **Socialization,** 209, 332 **Society,** 14,43 49, 51, 52, 54, 63, 72, 121, 122, 140, 147, 165, 269, 295, 297, 319 **Solution** , 13, 47, 60, 58, 60, 113, 116, 128, 129, 141, 196, 201, 213, 235, 261, 275,, 290, 300, 323, 324, 341 **Sorrow,** 10, 72, 78, 99, 100, 140 **Sorrow,** 225, 298, 329, 334 **Soul,** 75, 145, 180, 202, 341, 354, 365, 366 **Spirit Consciousness** , 82, 84, 86, 114, 123, 136, 288 **Spirit-Spiritual,** 49, 50, 57, 60, 63, 70, 81, 102, 104, 114, 115, 116, 117, 122, 151, 154, 161, 163, 165 171, 192, 194, 198, 202, 206, 247,273, 292, 295, 313, 328, 357 **SPIRITUAL: action,** 234, **alternative,** 234, **awakening,** 65, 217, 287, 312 **awareness,** 5, 84, 106 **being,** 252, 318 **blindless,** 48 **bonding,** 178 **condition,** 22, 53, 235, 249 **conditioning,** 295 **connection,** 5, 26, 186 **curiosity,** 171 **death,** 97, 132, 188, 21, **deficit,** 271, **effort,** 296, **energy,** 18, 56, 71, 241 **experience,** 156, 158, 230, 258, 324, 327 **growth,** 208, 295, 328, 341 **guidance,** 22, 23, 50, 53, 54, 66, 155, 117, 124, 137, 142, 143, 146, 228, 258, 266, 279, 285, 293 **guide,** 19 70, 77, 90, 112, 143, 157, 231, 236, 267, 305, 309, 343, 357 **healing,** 95, inner self, 5, 53, 67 **intelligence** 49, 247 **journey,** 27, 38, 54, 115, 117, 137, 277, 295 **Knowledge,** 38, 51, 127, 162, 224, 238 **malady,** 60, 89, 162 **message,** 4 **mosaic,** 168 **nourishment,** 340 **order,** 152, 172, 236, 283 **path,** 267, 327, 346 **practice,** 11, 15, 59, 70, 129, 136, 137, 140, 149, 201,211 212, 230, 231, 236, 238, 244, 247, 289, 323, 325, 330, 347, 348

principles, 199 **reality**, 49 recovery, 54, 144, 196, 199 **solution**, 39, 47, 53, 66, 143, 169, 200, 202, 203, 268, 311 **source**, 68, 149, 152, 164, 200, 299, 316, 349, 366 **substance** 101 **survival**, 354 **treatment**, 89, 201, 210, 211, 244, **understanding**, 89, 107, 112, 115, 151, 350, wealth, 271 **Spirituality**, 51, 117, 165, 241, 277 **Spiritually fit**, 25, 249 **Sponsor**, 160 **Stage**, 20, 26, 31, 54, 278 **STEPS: I**, 93, 337 **II**, 60, 338 **III**, 97, 339 **IV**, 99 **V**, 101, 217,345 **VI**, 103, 344 **VII**, 105, 345 **VIII**,108 **IX**, 109, 283, 342 **X**, 111 **XI**, 113 **XII**, 115, 350 **Stillness**, 7, 21, 22 , 135, 255, 333, 356 **Strategies**, 170 **Stress**, 269, 359 **Subconscious**, 4, 54, 89, 117, 159, 273, 287 **Success**, 78, 165 **Suffering**, 12, 22, 38, 50, 82, 83, 119, 122, 125, 131, 137, 161, 170, 200, 231, 234, 247, 250, 251, 253, 293 304, 313 **Suggestions**, 201, 202, 255, 363, 373 **Superiority**,63 89, 92, 168, 248, 270, **Support Group**, 102 **Suppress**, 44 **Surrender**, 6, 19, 34, 38, 61, 64, 70, 98, 117, 142, 151, 152, 153, 164, 192, 207, 229, 241, 247, 273, 293, 307, 311, 328, 363, 365 **Survival (instinct)**, 19, 96, 211 **Symptom**, 337 **Taking Suggestions**, 202 **Teacher**, 76, 121, 205, 67, 270, 304, 306, 360 **Temptation**, 154, 170, 321 **This too shall pass**, 6 **Thorough**, 99, 107, 109, 343 **Thoughts,** 56, 67, 84, 99, 102, 107, 111, 112, 124, 131, 167, 195, 204, 242, 257, 265, 274, 288, 308, Time, 113, 146, 150, 266 **Timing (perfect)**, 62, 76, 164, 293 **Tiny flame** , 353 **To Be**, 7 **Tolerance**, 12, 25, 41, 77, 134, 137, 148, 250, 341, 364 **Toolbox (Recovery)**, 33, 39, 338 **Torment**, 131, 138, 227, 304 **Train the mind** , 7, **Trance**, 27, 90 **Tranquility**, 77, 94, 130, 241 **Transformation**, 107, 110, 117, 127, 132, 185, 186 **Transient being**, 182, 194, 212, 313 **Transparency**, 212 **Treatment**, 206 **Trigger** 67, 132, 140, 159, 227, 238, 183, 249, 315 **True self**, 65, 254, 257, 282, 302 **Trust,** 70, 118, 122, 125, 139, 157, 100, 268, 304 **Truth**, 15, 17 20, 26, 27, 30, 38, 44, 54, 63, 82, 91, 92, 101, 104, 116, 144, 176 184, 213, 215, 222, 227, 238, 268, 285, 304, 319, 336, 346, 365 **Turmoil**, 39, 41, 62, 77, 304 **Turning the other cheek,** 331 **Twelve Step Program** , 160, 232, 277 **Twelve Steps**, 160, 213, 232 **Unappreciated**, 184, **Unbelief**, 110, 328 **Unconsciously**, 87, 137 **Unconditional love**,43, 353, 358 **Understanding**, 40, 50, 127, 134, 141, 164, 167, 215 **Inexplainable**, 56, 57, 59 **Unique**, 11, 20, 58, 83, 178, 200, 259, 293 **Unity**, 35, 241 **Unknown**, 8, 147, 301, 315, 339 **Unmanageable**, 281, 311, 338 **Unprejudiced**, 133 **Unrealistic**, 297 **Unrest, inner**, 129 **Untrained mind**, 7 **Usefulness** , 104 **Validation** , 32, 88, 264, 302, 322 **Value**, 35 **Values**, 261, **Vengeance**, 41 **Victim**, 94, 135, 211, 303, 323

Vigilance, 37, 90, 105, 154, 215, 218, 224, 336 **Virus of the mind**, 102, 120, 186 **Voice, A**, 35, 41, 55, 131, 195 **Void**, 26, 58, 151, 180, 271, 275, 278, 290, 326, 352 **Vulnerability**, 20, 30, 140, 229 **Walkabout**, 172 **Watcher**, 246, 308 **We**, 200, 232 **Whisper, the** , 18, 22, 62, 138, 179, 309 **Whole, spiritually** 20 **Will, His**, 28, 48, 70, 111, 112, 139, 216, 219, 223, 251, 252, 268, 283 **Will, ours**, 34, 37, 83, 98, 116, 120, 166, 172, 189, 214, 224, 240, 245, 248, 252, 261, 311, 363 **Willingness**, 9, 39, 40, 48, 58, 65, 113, 115, 175, 196, 197, 212, 255, 283, 291, 299, 304, 343, 351, 362 **Winner looser**, 175, 263, 265 **Wisdom**, 21, 48, 138, 176, 299 **Wise**, 42 **Worry**, 7, 8 , 16, 100, 107, 175, 255, 339, 364 **Worship**, 5, 68 **Worth, self**, 175, 259, 322 Wounding, 87, 141, 266 **Wreckage, of past**, 40, 61, 72, 250 **Wrongs**, 3, 17, 39, 103, 107, 109, 123, 124, 283, 285, 291, 306, 329, 344
Yeshua, 360 **Youth**, 159

About Author

Pedro has over two decades of personal and professional experience in substance abuse and recovery. His work has long been dedicated to supporting individuals and families as they navigate the fragile and transformative path of early recovery.

His literary journey begins here, with future projects already underway exploring healing, Truth, and the strength of the human spirit.

Stay connected—visit thejourneyofrecovery.com to explore his latest work and upcoming releases. You can also find him on Instagram @thejourneyofrecovery1999 and other social platforms as they grow